IN AND AROUND
LONDON FOR KIDS

CONTENTS

INTRODUCTION

'I'm bored, Mum!' All parents with children old enough to talk will have heard this familiar battle cry at one time or another. Designed to exasperate all but the stalwart, most of us will eventually succumb – usually in the school holidays – and an 'outing' will occur, preferably somewhere that offers something for the grown-ups too. Perhaps our trips started like this, although, I suspect, we ventured forth long before our first-born was old enough to speak the dreaded words. Anyway, what started as an occasional entertainment has taken us to numerous venues over the years as inevitably a visit to one place would result in us acquiring several leaflets promoting others and most weekends will find us out and about in what has become a genuine pleasure – exploring the wealth of places to visit in, around and within reach of London.

As the children have grown older we have ventured further afield and our definition of 'within reach of London' is anywhere that we can drive to and back from in a day, having enjoyed ourselves in between. If your children are like ours and enjoy travelling, they will enjoy the getting there as much as the destination. So you will find more here than just the more obvious entries in central London, although many of those are covered too.

What does become apparent after not too many of these outings is that small things help a visit with children to go much more smoothly, especially where there is a baby or toddlers in tow. We found quite a difference in the standard of facilities in places, even in those aimed specifically at children. I have, therefore, paid particular attention to wheel-friendliness, catering and baby-changing facilities. Incidentally, I have a personal dislike of self-service catering since if visiting as a lone parent I have yet to discover a way of carrying a laden tray, holding on to a wayward toddler *and* pushing a buggy, all at the same time, without disastrous consequences. I have not allowed this to cloud my judgement since almost all places would be disqualified under this criterion.

All the entries in the book have been personally visited by us and are featured because they offer value-for-money; do not infer 'cheap' from this because many places – particularly in central London – are not necessarily so, but if they are here it is because I feel that they offer a lot for the money you pay. Although most of the obvious venues in central London are included in this guide, it is not designed to be an exhaustive guide to every attraction in the capital but a selection of those we consider the best. Many more than are listed here were visited and rejected for a variety of reasons.

Many of the places have holiday activity programmes for children or special events all year round, but they are too variable to be included in this book. It is certainly worth calling in advance to check the programme timetable since coinciding a visit with one of these may well add extra-entertainment value to the visit.

Where a listing has seasonal opening hours do call and check exact dates as these can also vary from year to year.

ARUNDEL CASTLE

ARUNDEL, WEST SUSSEX, BN18 9AB
TEL: 01903 883136 / 01903 882173   FAX: 01903 884581

HOW LONG WILL WE SPEND THERE?
Allow three hours.

WHICH AGE GROUP WILL IT APPEAL TO?
All ages.

INTRODUCTION
A truly magnificent castle and, judging from the polyglot visitors, clearly a popular European tourist destination. All the more odd then to discover that the main reason for the long queue to get in was because the ticket office operates by issuing a sort of raffle ticket and is not automated in any way (no Switch or credit cards!). The castle itself is really very impressive. Built at the end of the 11th century by Roger de Montgomery, Earl of Arundel, it has been the seat of the Dukes of Norfolk and Earls of Arundel for over 700 years and is still occupied by the present Duke and his family. This castle is no ruin with its intact moat, drawbridge and portcullis to the entire immaculate interior. The rooms are filled with treasures, fine furniture and portraits and there is plenty to occupy curious minds, especially with the help of the 'young person's guide' which at £1.80 offers excellent value. Although the guide is aimed at the 8–14 age group it is full of information and questions on each room, pictures to colour and general historical facts. It's not advertised anywhere so head for the shop (or the bookstall in the Baron's Hall) to get a copy. The armoury has its usual attraction for small boys but all the rooms are splendid – look out for Mary, Queen of Scots' prayer book and rosary and the nine-foot-thick walls in the oldest part of the castle. The grounds are not extensive and consist mostly of lawns. You can also visit the Fitzalan Chapel which is the private

11

burial chapel of the Dukes and Earls. Interestingly, the Roman Catholic chapel directly adjoins the Anglican parish church of Arundel and, although they are physically connected, there is no access from one to the other. Those feeling fit can climb the 120 steps to the top of the keep for views of the Isle of Wight.

HOW TO GET THERE AND WHERE TO PARK:

Car: Situated four miles north of Littlehampton on the A27. Pay-and-display car-park at the foot of the castle with a five-minute steep walk up the hill or use the free castle car-park – but beware, there are often long queues to get in.

Train: Frequent train service from London Victoria. The castle is a ten-minute walk from Arundel station.

OPENING HOURS

1 April until the last Friday in October, Sunday to Friday, 12–5 p.m. (Last admission 4 p.m.) N.B. If Easter falls before 1 April the castle will be open on Easter Sunday.
Closed: Saturdays and Good Friday.

ADMISSION

Adults: £5.50. Children (5–15): £4. Senior citizens: £5. Family tickets (two adults and up to two children): £15. Under-fives: free.
Grounds, Keep and Fitzalan Chapel only: £2.

WHEELCHAIR AND PUSHCHAIR ACCESS

Separate entrance for wheelchairs and the castle is fully accessible to standard-size wheelchairs and pushchairs.

REFRESHMENTS

The tea-garden is quite a trek from the castle and is rather disappointing; conjuring up images of home cooking it is, in fact, a kiosk selling vending-machine drinks and packaged muffins – albeit in a beautiful garden setting. They do have fresh scones but with packaged jam and no cream – too early in the day, apparently! No indoor seating and no high-chairs. The castle's licensed restaurant serves adequate but not wildly exciting fare – soup and roll £2.30, baked potatoes from £2.20, chicken pie £2.50. Children's meals available and two high-chairs. Picnics can be enjoyed on the lawns.

SHOP
Located on the ground floor, it has a super selection in both the gift area and the pantry section which is packed with good things to eat and drink.

TOILET FACILITIES
Toilets in the castle have wheelchair access but there are no purpose-built baby-changing facilities – although the stone shelf in the ladies' could be used for changing nappies. Toilets at the tea-garden have wheelchair access but no baby-changing facilities.

CLOAKROOM
Unsupervised area for leaving pushchairs and coats.

PHOTOGRAPHY
Not allowed in the castle.

DOGS
Guide dogs only.

BEKONSCOT MODEL VILLAGE

WARWICK ROAD, BEACONSFIELD, BUCKINGHAMSHIRE, HP9 2PL
TEL/FAX: 01494 672919

HOW LONG SHOULD WE SPEND THERE?
Allow one hour.

WHICH AGE GROUP WILL IT APPEAL TO?
Suitable for all ages.

INTRODUCTION
Bekonscot claims to be the oldest model village in the world and is certainly one of the most charming. It is set in one and a half acres of carefully tended landscaped gardens, which are beautiful in themselves, with numerous miniature shrubs and bright displays of seasonal flowers, the 1930s village is attentive to detail and only lacks in authenticity if you feel that there is a limit to the number of castles and churches a small English village could support! Also depicted are railway stations, a lake with a working yacht, a football stadium, a town hall, a college, a pier, a racecourse, even an airfield and much, much more. Winding through myriad buildings is a splendid four-track outdoor model railway, but it's the surprises that delight, such as coming across the working steam-roller and hay baler or the anglers hidden in every stream and pond, one of which is home to an enormous carp which on a 1:1 scale would be the size of a blue whale.

Brochures for £1 and children's quiz sheets for 10p are available at the ticket office located in an old railway carriage as you enter.

Enid Blyton once lived close by and the model village is reckoned by experts to have been the inspiration for her Noddy stories and, therefore, the original Toytown.

HOW TO GET THERE AND WHERE TO PARK

Car: Leave the M40 at junction 2 and follow the brown tourist signs. Be careful not to miss the final sign off the main road. There's a pay-and-display car-park which is free on Sundays and bank holidays and a main car-park opposite the entrance.

Train: Ten minutes' walk uphill from Beaconsfield station which is on the main Marylebone–Birmingham line.

OPENING HOURS

12 February to 30 October daily, 10 a.m.– 5 p.m.

PRICE

Adults: £3.20. Children (3–15): £1.60. Senior citizens, students and unemployed: £2.20. Family ticket (two adults and two children): £9 (with each additional child: £1.30). Under-threes: free.

WHEELCHAIR AND PUSHCHAIR ACCESS

Smooth, gently undulating but narrow footpaths, which can get very congested. Narrow wheelchairs are available. The only area not accessible to wheels is the raised walkway which gives a panoramic view of the site.

REFRESHMENTS

There is a snack bar open from 11 a.m. to 4 p.m. serving tea and coffee, cans and hot snacks. Sandwiches start at £1.20, crisps, wrapped cakes and hot snacks such as baked potatoes for £1.90 and pizza for £1.50. Expect no haute cuisine here (polystyrene rather than porcelain) but the food is adequate. There are lots of picnic tables and benches in the shade of a huge tree and a wooden shelter for rainy days. If there's no room here then you can head for the picnic room. Beaconsfield old town is about a mile away and looked promising for cream teas and pub lunches.

SHOP

Located in a railway carriage, it has a small selection of Thomas the Tank Engine merchandise, die-cast period cars, mugs and pocket-money toys and posters.

TOILET FACILITIES

Baby-changing facilities and wheelchair-access toilet.

CLOAKROOM
Not supervised, but you can leave things at your own risk in the stockroom.

PHOTOGRAPHY
Allowed and film sold in the shop.

DOGS
Guide dogs only.

HMS BELFAST

MORGANS LANE, TOOLEY STREET, LONDON, SE1 2JH
TEL: 0171 407 6434   FAX: 0171 403 0719

HOW LONG SHOULD WE SPEND THERE?
Allow a minimum of two hours.

WHICH AGE GROUP WILL IT APPEAL TO?
All ages.

INTRODUCTION
This is yet another Imperial War Museum success. As the leaflet says:
'HMS *Belfast* is the only surviving example of the great fleets of big-gun
armoured warships built for the Royal Navy in the first half of the
twentieth century.' Don't be deceived into thinking, as we did, that you are
in for a brief hour's visit; this World War II cruiser is enormous. Launched
in 1938 she served right through the war and the reconstructions inside
the ship are designed to recreate the atmosphere of life on board during
one of her three-month stints at sea. The operations room, for example,
captures the tension of the engagement with the German battle-cruiser
Scharnhorst at the Battle of North Cape and the forward mess decks use
models and sound effects to recreate the seeming boredom of the sailors as
they played cards or idled away the time at the tables or in hammocks
slung above them, those asleep and those awake sharing the same dimly lit
space. The punishment cell was clearly something to be avoided; up to 14
days confinement in a tiny room on strict rations, deprived of even the
most basic pastimes and with only a bible to read. Nor, for that matter, can
visits to the dentist's surgery or the sick-bay have been particularly happy
experiences. The free guide takes you expertly through the maze of the
ship's interior which is divided into eight colour-coded zones and which
covers seven decks – be prepared for vertical steps, abrupt door lips, low

17

doorways and cramped spaces. If you can then imagine the chaos and heat of battle – particularly while working in the claustrophobic engine rooms – it is easy to imagine how uncomfortable the conditions must have been for those on board and, as if this were not enough, the ship served on the terrible Arctic convoy route where the crew often had to endure temperatures of -30 degrees Centigrade.

There is a small area devoted to a static exhibition covering the ship's history and although there isn't much interactivity, the videos and commentaries help to explain certain sections and you can pretend to operate the light anti-aircraft guns. Armoury of course plays a large part in the ship's history and is a big attraction for the children; there are four heavily armoured shell rooms holding over 50 shells each in order to service the 32 guns – some of which had a firing range of 14 miles – and others had the capacity of firing up to 240 rounds per minute.

HOW TO GET THERE AND WHERE TO PARK
Car: There is a car- and coach-park on Tooley Street after Morgans Lane and before Tower Bridge which charges £5 for the day at weekends.
Underground: A 15-minute walk from London Bridge station (Northern line).
Train: A 15-minute walk from London Bridge station.
Boat: Every 15 to 30 minutes from 11 a.m.–5 p.m. (from Easter to the end of October) to Butlers Wharf, Tower pier and London Bridge city pier.

OPENING HOURS
1 March to 31 October, daily, 10 a.m.–6 p.m. (last admission 5.15 p.m.).
1 November to 28/29 February, daily, 10 a.m.–5 p.m. (last admission 4.15 p.m.).
Closed: 24–26 December.

ADMISSION
Adults: £4.40. Children (5–16): £2.20. Senior citizens, students and unemployed: £3.30. Family ticket: one child has free entry for every family of two adults and two children. *Disabled visitors*: Adults: £2.20. Children (5–16): £1.10. All other concessions: £1.65. Under-fives: free of charge.

WHEELCHAIR AND PUSHCHAIR ACCESS
Not really suitable for pushchairs. There is partial access for wheelchairs onto the main deck and ramps give access to the upper (no. 2) deck with the canteen, sick-bay, operating theatre, dental surgery and other areas dedicated more to everyday life on board rather than to battle action area

– but there are many parts of the ship which would be impossible to reach.

REFRESHMENTS
The Walrus café serves very basic food, but is a warm sanctuary when the wind is whipping off the Thames. They have a small selection of biscuits and cakes from 80p to £1.35, sandwiches from £2.50 to £2.85, and baguettes from £3 to £3.35. There's a children's pick 'n' mix box at £2.25 and hot food, such as sausages or chicken nuggets, which is served until 3 p.m. Tea is 75p, coffee is 90p, soft drinks from 80p to £1.30. We spotted one high-chair. There is nowhere on board for picnics but there are benches along the riverside with spectacular views, as well as a selection of restaurants at the nearby Hays Galleria and if you're feeling flush some upmarket restaurants at Butlers Wharf.

SHOP
There is a small shop by the entrance on the riverbank selling books and other merchandise with nautical and wartime themes, upmarket gifts and pocket-money toys.

TOILET FACILITIES
There are baby-changing facilities and wheelchair-access toilets on the quarterdeck near the main entrance. These are kept locked for some inexplicable reason so an attendant has to be found before you can gain access.

CLOAKROOM
Pushchairs can be left unsupervised by the main entrance, but there are no facilities for bags.

PHOTOGRAPHY
Allowed throughout the ship.

DOGS
Only guide dogs are allowed on board and the staff prefer prior warning.

BETHNAL GREEN
MUSEUM OF
CHILDHOOD

CAMBRIDGE HEATH ROAD, LONDON, E2 9PA
TEL: 0181 980 4315/0181 980 3204/0181 980 2415

HOW LONG SHOULD WE SPEND THERE?
Allow one to two hours.

WHICH AGE GROUP WILL IT APPEAL TO?
Suitable for over-fives.

INTRODUCTION
This is a vast museum housing one of the world's largest collection of toys, doll's-houses and games and, being free, offers excellent value. However, it is strangely lacking in interactive displays and we found the children tired of the many glass-cased exhibits before we had seen even a small part of the museum. The displays seem rather detached from the children themselves and are more about children as social comments on the periods with which they are associated rather than for children. That said, there are Saturday and holiday workshops and shows, and paper and pencils for drawing or for using at the workshops are available on request. Perhaps the best way to approach this museum is not to try and do it all in one day, but to make several visits and concentrate on only one area at a time. They have a huge section on dolls arranged chronologically from 1680 to modern-day Barbies and ethnic dolls. There are masses of games, twentieth-century learning toys, over 40 doll's-houses, teddy bears, toy soldiers, trains and puppets. In the childhood gallery in the upper gallery, you will find an interesting exhibition following the life of a child over

different historical periods. There are some fascinating exhibits including sixteenth-century swaddling bands, eighteenth-century prams, rattles, feeding bottles, Victorian underwear all the way through to twentieth-century adolescent toys. A good museum for a wet day.

HOW TO GET THERE AND WHERE TO PARK

Car: There are 12 free places on the museum forecourt but if these are full, which they invariably are, then you will have to use nearby roads for parking. Not always easy.

Underground: Bethnal Green station five minutes' walk.

Train: Cambridge Heath station 10 minutes' walk.

OPENING HOURS

All year, Monday to Saturday (excluding Friday), 10 a.m–5.50 p.m. Sunday 2.30 p.m.–5.50 p.m.

Closed: Fridays, 1 January, May bank holiday, 24–26 December.

ADMISSION

Free, although some holiday and weekend shows are subject to a fee.

WHEELCHAIR AND PUSHCHAIR ACCESS

Once on the main floors, access is fine and there are ramps to the lower gallery but there are steps from the ground floor to the upper gallery. Help can be arranged for wheelchair users if you call in advance (tel: 0181 980 3204/4315) but you could find it a little difficult with a pushchair.

REFRESHMENTS

A light and spacious café located on the ground floor serves good quality food with a special children's mini-sandwich platter at £1.20, baby food at £1 and the staff are happy to warm a baby's bottle. Coffee is 80p, tea 70p and orange juice 80p. We spotted four high-chairs and they have thoughtfully provided a plan and drawing area for younger visitors. The café is open weekdays from 11 a.m. to 4 p.m., Saturdays and holidays from 10 a.m. to 5 p.m. and Sundays from 2.30 p.m. to 5 p.m. The museum was busy the day we visited and there were long queues at the self-service counter. It is acceptable to have your own food but you may prefer to picnic in the museum grounds or adjoining park. No food is allowed in the galleries.

SHOP

Located on the ground floor, the shop is rather small but it sells books, stickers, some interesting colour-in posters which are related to museum exhibits and a museum guidebook.

TOILET FACILITIES
Separate wheelchair-access toilet. No specific baby-changing facilities but a chair and table were available in the ladies' toilet.

CLOAKROOM
There is an unsupervised area with room for pushchairs and left-luggage lockers which cost £1.

PHOTOGRAPHY
Allowed but no film sold.

DOGS
Guide dogs only.

THE BLUEBELL RAILWAY

SHEFFIELD PARK STATION, EAST SUSSEX, TN22 3QL
TEL: TIMETABLE INFORMATION 01825 722370 (24 HOURS)/ADVANCE
BOOKINGS 01825 722008/GENERAL ENQUIRIES 01825 723777
FAX: 01825 724139

HOW LONG SHOULD WE SPEND THERE?
Allow two hours.

WHICH AGE GROUP WILL IT APPEAL TO?
Suitable for all ages.

INTRODUCTION
I'm not a great lover of railways other than as a practical mode of transport but I do understand that the smell of steam engines has a certain allure for some, amongst whom can be included most small children. As railways go the Bluebell is better than most we have visited, not least because the time you can spend riding on the steam engines themselves is extensive and there is not such a heavy emphasis on engine sheds and engines in various stages of disrepair. The Victorian station itself is a treat in its attention to detail and the carriages have been lovingly restored from the private first-class to the observation carriage from the Ffestiniog railway. The superb-looking 1920s Pullman carriage has to be pre-booked for Saturday dinner or Sunday lunch. Allow one and a half hours for the round trip to Kingscote from Sheffield Park but we opted to stop at the halfway point, Horsted Keynes, which takes just 15 minutes one way and you can cross over the platform and get a return train almost immediately. This 1930s station is said to be one of the finest examples of station preservation in the country. Chugging along through the countryside with a gentle breeze

blowing through the open windows on a hot summer's day really is very restful, it's a pity it doesn't have the same soporific effect on the children.

HOW TO GET THERE AND WHERE TO PARK

Car: Follow signs for Sheffield Park Station which is situated on the A275 East Grinstead–Lewes main road, two miles north of the junction with the A272 from where it is signposted. There are three car-parks: one at the entrance, one closer to the station and an overspill across the road from the entrance. There is no road access to Kingscote Station and if you start your journey here you must park your car at East Grinstead and take the vintage bus service from the station forecourt or from the High Street.

Train: You can book direct to the Bluebell Railway from London Victoria. Your ticket will include a train to East Grinstead, the vintage bus transfer (as described above) and a Bluebell Railway trip.

OPENING HOURS

Open all year with erratic opening days and three complicated programmes of services so best to call first.

ADMISSION

Sheffield Park to Horsted Keynes
First class:
Single – adult: £5. Children (3–15): £2.50.
Return – adult: £7.60. Children (3–15): £3.80.
Third class:
Single – adult: £3. Children (3–15): £1.50.
Return – adult: £5.60. Children (3–15): £2.80.
Family ticket (two adults and up to three children): £15.
Senior citizens: £4.80.

Sheffield Park to Kingscote
First class:
Single – adult: £6. Children (3–15): £3.
Return – adult: £10. Children (3–15): £5.
Third class:
Single – adult: £4. Children (3–15): £2.
Return – adult: £7.20. Children (3–15): £3.60.
Family ticket (two adults and up to three children): £19.50.
Senior citizens: £6.
Dogs and buggies: 50p.

WHEELCHAIR AND PUSHCHAIR ACCESS

Easy access to Sheffield Park station and a ramp is provided for access to the trains themselves; buggies should then be left by the door. A delightfully helpful member of staff advised us that they would carry wheelchairs upstairs to the Puffers restaurant, but this is not really necessary since the Bessemer Arms is warm and welcoming.

REFRESHMENTS

There is normally a carriage selling drinks and snacks on the train journey. There is an ice-cream and snack kiosk on the platform and for something more substantial venture into the Bessemer Arms bar which welcomes children and serves good-value fare; home-made soup and roll £2.10, grilled rib-eye steak £6.95, Cumberland sausage £4.95, mushroom and tomato quiche £4.50. Colouring pads and crayons are thoughtfully provided. There are two outside eating areas and upstairs there's a self-service restaurant called Puffers. High-chairs available.

SHOP

Trains, trains and more trains! Pick up anything you need on the subject of railways, trains and Thomas the Tank Engine.

TOILET FACILITIES

Near entrance, Victorian and spartan with a table for baby-changing. Toilets inside the Bessemer Arms are more comfortable with proper changing facilities. Wheelchair access to both.

CLOAKROOM

No.

PHOTOGRAPHY

Allowed and film sold.

DOGS

Guide dogs only.

BOAT TRIP ON THE THAMES

**GREENWICH CATAMARAN CRUISERS, CHARING CROSS PIER,
VICTORIA EMBANKMENT, LONDON, WC2N 6NU.
TEL: 0171 987 1185 (RECORDED INFORMATION)/0171 839 3572
FAX: 0171 839 1034**

HOW LONG SHOULD WE SPEND THERE?
The trip takes an hour (one way) but you can make this an all-day excursion.

WHICH AGE GROUP WILL IT APPEAL TO?
Suitable for all ages.

INTRODUCTION
It is a delight to travel to Greenwich by boat down the Thames. Buy your ticket at Charing Cross pier office just 100 yards beyond the pier itself on the Embankment and then you may have a slight wait for the 'boat', which is actually a catamaran. We chose a hot, breezy day and boarded the vessel with some trepidation but we couldn't feel any swell at all and were well sheltered from the wind by the glass sides. The roof was open but can be closed to give full protection on a rainy day. You can pick up a free colour map on board but this isn't nearly as informative as the humorous commentary given by one of the crew (not a qualified guide) who, as well as the obvious stuff, gives out all sorts of gratuitous but nonetheless entertaining snippets of information. After passing such landmarks as St Paul's Cathedral, the new Globe Theatre, the Tower of London, Tower Bridge, HMS *Belfast*, Canary Wharf and many more on the hour-long trip, you can disembark at Greenwich pier (after stopping at the Tower of London) and while away some time before the return trip or make a full

day of it by experiencing some of the many attractions in the historical town.

HOW TO GET THERE AND WHERE TO PARK

Car: Parking is limited but free on the Embankment on Sundays.
Underground: A five-minute walk from Embankment station or ten minutes from Charing Cross.
Train: Ten minutes' walk from Charing Cross station.

OPENING HOURS

Daily, April to October, every 30 minutes, 10.30 a.m.–4 p.m.
Daily, November to March, every 45 minutes, 10.30 a.m.–4 p.m.

ADMISSION

From Charing Cross to Greenwich via the Tower of London and St Katherine's Dock – Adults: £6 single, £7 return. Children (under 16 years): £3.50 single, £3.80 return. Ten per cent reduction for senior citizens, students, wheelchair users and carers.

WHEELCHAIR AND PUSHCHAIR ACCESS

Full access for wheelchairs. Pushchairs can be managed with care.

REFRESHMENTS

Soft drinks, beer and a limited range of snacks served on board. There is a café at Greenwich Pier.

SHOP

No shop on board but shops on the pier and in Greenwich.

TOILET FACILITIES

Toilets available on board but no baby-changing facilities.

CLOAKROOM

No.

PHOTOGRAPHY

Allowed but no film sold on board.

DOGS

Small dogs allowed if kept on a lead and under control.

BRITAIN AT WAR EXPERIENCE

TOOLEY STREET, LONDON, SE1
TEL: 0171 403 3171

HOW LONG SHOULD WE SPEND THERE?
Allow one hour.

WHICH AGE GROUP WILL IT APPEAL TO?
Suitable for over-fives.

INTRODUCTION
A small museum that manages to evoke the feeling of war-torn Britain during the Second World War. Stepping into a lift you are transported back to a London Underground tunnel that is serving as a bomb shelter in the 1940s. There is a video to set the scene and lots of authentic background noise. If this scenario is popular with the children then you can experience more of the same inside a darkened Anderson shelter during a bombing raid, which includes the particularly ominous sound of the 'Doodlebug'. The mannequins could do with a touch of renovation here and there but the use of the front pages of newspapers, posters and memorabilia help to recreate the scene. I think much of it was lost on the younger visitors, although the concept of rationed food seemed to strike a nerve and the gasmasks excited considerable interest. The best bit by far is the reconstructed bombed-out street at night-time where a truly inspired touch is to include a ladies' outfitters in the scenario resulting in gruesomely arranged limbs strewn around the bombsite looking suspiciously like bits of bodies, much to the children's horror and delight! You don't get the impression that they have huge funds at their disposal but the rather Heath Robinson feel to the place only seems to add to the atmosphere.

HOW TO GET THERE AND WHERE TO PARK

Car: Large car-park at the London Bridge end of Tooley Street or on-street parking at weekends.

Underground: A few minutes' walk from London Bridge station.

Train: As above.

OPENING HOURS

October to end-March, daily, 10 a.m.–4.30 p.m.

April to end-September, daily, 10 a.m.–5.30 p.m.

Closed: 24–26 December.

ADMISSION

Adults: £5.95. Children (5–16): £2.95. Senior citizens and students: £3.95. Family ticket (two adults and two children): £14. Wheelchair users and under-fives: free. Carers: £3.95.

WHEELCHAIR AND PUSHCHAIR ACCESS

Full access.

REFRESHMENTS

None on site but lots of possibilities in the immediate vicinity with perhaps the best selection in the Hays Galleria opposite. There is also the pleasurable option of eating a picnic by the river.

SHOP

A small, sparsely stocked shop with one or two books on the period, pick 'n' mix sweets, key rings, tapes (£3.99) and CDs (£5.99) of music from the 1940s.

TOILET FACILITIES

No baby-changing or wheelchair facilities.

CLOAKROOM

Staff in the entrance kiosk will store things for you.

PHOTOGRAPHY

Allowed but no film sold.

DOGS

Guide dogs only.

THE BRITISH MUSEUM

GREAT RUSSELL STREET, LONDON, WC1B 3DG
TEL: 0171 636 1555/0171 580 1788 /0171 637 7384
WEBSITE – HTTP://WWW.BRITISH@MUSEUM.AC.UK

HOW LONG SHOULD WE SPEND THERE?
Allow two and a half hours.

WHICH AGE GROUP WILL IT APPEAL TO?
Suitable for over-fives.

INTRODUCTION
A huge array of 4,000 artefacts showing the works of man from pre-history to the present day are displayed in a massive, imposing building which originally housed the British Library – the Library is now being transferred to its new site at St Pancras. Consequently when we visited there was a degree of reorganisation going on and, given that there is a constant programme of gallery redevelopment anyway, some areas were a little disappointing. For example, some of the Egyptology galleries on the upper floor were inaccessible. Nonetheless there were several mummified bodies to satisfy the ghoulish fascination and plenty of beautifully decorated coffins and sarcophagi. This section is undoubtedly the most fascinating for small children, together with the Egyptian sculptures on the ground floor which command attention by virtue of their huge scale. The Lindow Man is a close second in the gruesome stakes, especially since the method of his killing is described in graphic detail; the hologram of his head is a nice touch although all galleries cry out for updating with more interactivity and videos and more back-up; photographs of the tomb sites and excavations in Egypt, for instance, would have helped enormously to

set the exhibits in context. It seems mean-spirited to criticise when the museum is free and everything is signed in great detail but, while being extremely informative and imposing in size and sheer number of exhibits, it remains very static and scholarly – especially for children who have a short attention span. Some effort in this direction has been made and we picked up quiz sheets for kids at the information desk which helped to enliven the Mexican gallery and the Money gallery (these weren't advertised anywhere and we wouldn't have known about them if we hadn't asked). There is also a standard museum guide on sale at £3 and a map/tour guide for £1 available at the gift shop in the main entrance hall. There are guided tours lasting 90 minutes starting at 10.45 a.m. from Monday to Saturday and at 3 p.m. on Sundays; these can be booked at the gift shop but the ones we saw were very adult. Don't try to do it all in one visit – we were there for two and a half hours and still only saw four galleries, but that was enough.

The museum was very busy and it is advisable to avoid Sundays when a lot of visiting tour groups drop in. A queue tends to build up before opening time, so be prepared for a ten- to 15-minute wait outdoors. The world-famous Reading Room has now closed pending its future conversion to a public-access library and there is also further development of the surrounding terrace into a glass-roofed restaurant.

HOW TO GET THERE AND WHERE TO PARK
Car: Not easy to park but if you're determined there's a car-park under Bloomsbury Square or meter-parking in surrounding streets (free on Sundays).
Underground: Holborn, Tottenham Court Road or Russell Square stations.
Train: 30 minutes' walk from Euston station or take the underground to any of the stations listed above.

OPENING HOURS
All year, Monday to Saturday, 10 a.m.–5 p.m.
Sunday, 2.30 p.m. to 6 p.m.
Closed: 1 January, 10 April, 5 May, 24–26 December.

ADMISSION
Free, but a donation of at least £2 per visitor is requested.

WHEELCHAIR AND PUSHCHAIR ACCESS
Don't be put off by the steep flight of stairs at the entrance; there is a wheelchair lift to the right – ring the bell and a warden will operate it for

you. Once inside almost all areas are accessible with lifts to all floors and a dedicated wheelchair lift at the rear of the building in gallery 34. The café is easily accessible but the restaurant is reached by a steep flight of steps. A warden will escort you to a rear entrance on request.

REFRESHMENTS
Exceptional quality catering in the restaurant but at a high price; salmon in sour cream and dill £7.95, roast red peppers with fennel and goats' cheese £5.75, spiced chicken with yoghurt £6.95, broccoli and potato soup with a roll £2.95. There are sandwiches on offer too at £2.65 but even these have such creative fillings that you may struggle to find something for simple childish tastes. There are glorious cakes from £3, fruit salad for £3.25, but even the tea and coffee are expensive at £1.20 and £1.45 respectively and a glass of Coke is an exorbitant £1.20. Afternoon tea consisting of a sandwich, cake, scone, jam and cream is £4.95. We had considerable difficulty finding a table but this may be because the adjacent café was closed (no one seemed to know why). There were two high-chairs.

SHOP
The children's bookshop located in gallery 26 is a gem of originality with wonderful souvenirs such as mummies' coffin pencil tins; bronze Egyptian ornamental weights for £2.99; replica Roman coin sets for £1; Roman coin badges for £1; Egyptian face masks; British Museum colouring books and activity books relating to different civilisations for £2.50.

TOILET FACILITIES
Plenty of toilets – all situated on the ground floor – with wheelchair access off gallery 25 and 26. Baby-changing facilities off gallery 25.

CLOAKROOM
Supervised cloakroom Monday to Saturday, 10 a.m.–4.30 p.m. and Sunday, 2.30 p.m.– 5.30 p.m.

PHOTOGRAPHY
Photography allowed in all areas except where indicated (no tripods allowed anywhere). Film sold in gift shop.

DOGS
Guide dogs only.

BUCKINGHAMSHIRE RAILWAY CENTRE

QUAINTON ROAD STATION, QUAINTON, NR AYLESBURY, BUCKS, HP22 4BY
TEL: 01 296 655450 (RECORDED INFORMATION SERVICE)/01 296 655720

HOW LONG SHOULD WE SPEND THERE?
The amount of time to allow depends on which of the many different programmes are running on the day you visit.

WHICH AGE GROUP WILL IT APPEAL TO?
Suitable for all ages.

INTRODUCTION
An unsophisticated, peculiarly English place, run with all the enthusiasm that genuine railway buffs can muster. It's worth checking out the special event days; we joined the Santa's Magic Steaming ride, a package which included reserved seats on the steam train (a slightly disappointing 30-minute ride which involved steaming backwards and forwards over the same half mile of track), a present for each of the children, given out on the train by Father Christmas and seasonal refreshments served in the converted railway carriage followed by a magic show (popular, so book early). A normal steaming day would allow you to explore the 25 acres of railway history. You enter through the disused Victorian country station and are then at liberty to roam around the collection of locomotives, carriages and wagons – including exhibits from South Africa and America dating back to the 1870s – and there are free steam-train rides. Crossing the footbridge you can visit the gift and bookshop, second-hand bookshop and the very small museum/maintenance shed where you can take a brief ride on the miniature railway or there is a more extensive version to be found beyond the restoration shed in the up yard. On special event days,

Easter and bank holidays, there is always a host of other things going on, like circus displays, car rallies, bus and traction-engine displays.

HOW TO GET THERE AND WHERE TO PARK

Car: Signposted off the A41 Aylesbury–Bicester road at Waddesdon and off the A413 Buckingham–Aylesbury road at Whitchurch – follow the brown signs. Junctions 7, 8 and 9 of the M40 are all close by. Lots of free parking.

Bus: Regular bus service from Aylesbury bus station to Quainton on Saturdays and Wednesdays. For more information call: 01296 23445.

OPENING HOURS

Static viewing days (train rides not available) on Saturdays.

Steaming days (with train rides) start Easter Sunday and then every Sunday and bank holiday until the end of October.

Special event days programme (Thomas the Tank Engine and Santa days) – apply for leaflet or phone for full details.

All open on Saturday, Sunday and some Wednesdays during the summer, 11 a.m.–6 p.m. (5 p.m. on Wednesdays). Last admission one hour before closing.

Closed: October–Easter (although sometimes open for special events).

ADMISSION

Static days: Adults: £2. Children (over five) and pensioners: £1. No family ticket.

Steaming days: Adults: £3.50. Children (over five) and pensioners: £2.50. Family ticket (two adults and up to four children): £10.

bank holidays: Adults: £4.50. Children (over five) and pensioners: £3. Family ticket (two adults and up to four children): £14.

Special prices apply on Thomas the Tank Engine and Santa days. Call for details.

WHEELCHAIR AND PUSHCHAIR ACCESS

There is access to the major part of the site including the train ride and the miniature railway. The only inaccessible areas are some parts of the engine sheds and some old carriages.

REFRESHMENTS

Fairly basic fare served inside a converted railway carriage. It is not accessible to wheelchairs and buggies but there are lots of tables outside, some of which are under cover. There are also plenty of picnic benches around the site.

SHOP
There is a small shop in one of the buildings that sells railway-related gifts and the inevitable Thomas the Tank Engine merchandise. There is also a second-hand bookshop.

TOILET FACILITIES
Wheelchair-accessible toilets and baby-changing facilities available.

CLOAKROOM
No.

PHOTOGRAPHY
Allowed.

DOGS
Allowed if on lead.

CABINET WAR ROOMS

CLIVE STEPS, KING CHARLES STREET, LONDON, SW1A 2AQ
TEL: 0171 930 6961 FAX: 0171 839 5897

HOW LONG SHOULD WE SPEND THERE?
Allow one hour.

WHICH AGE GROUP WILL IT APPEAL TO?
Suitable for over-fives.

INTRODUCTION
A potentially dull experience for the children is transformed by the issue of free personal Acoustiguides (a device rather like a large mobile phone) to all visitors which give a tape-recorded, room-by-room commentary interspersed with first-hand accounts of personal war experiences and Churchill's speeches. What you see are the 21 basement rooms of a government building converted into emergency underground accommodation for the Prime Minister and key members of the Cabinet and war staff as the Second World War broke out. It doesn't sound very captivating in essence but these rooms – ranging from the scene-setting introductory area to the sleeping quarters and operational rooms, which were the nerve centre of the War Cabinet – have been faithfully restored in minute detail, to the condition in which they would have been during the war, by the Imperial War Museum; in some cases, such as the Map Room, the rooms you see today are the actual rooms as they were on the day that the last man put out the lights and locked the door. Together with the informative commentary and sound effects they really succeed in evoking the tense and frenetic atmosphere that must have pervaded these rooms during the six years of the war.

HOW TO GET THERE AND WHERE TO PARK
Car: Car-park in Great College Street.
Underground: A five-minute walk from Westminster station.
Train: Victoria station then underground to Westminster station.
Entrance is on Horse Guards Road overlooking St James's Park.

OPENING HOURS
October to end-March, daily, 10 a.m.–6 p.m.
April to end-September, daily, 9.30 a.m.–6 p.m.
Last admission 5.15 p.m.
Closed: 25–26 December

ADMISSION
Adults: £4.40. Children (5–16): £2.20. Senior citizens and students: £3.30.
Registered unemployed: £2.20. Family ticket (minimum one adult and two
children): full price but one child admitted free so two adults and two
children costs £11. Registered disabled: half-price.

WHEELCHAIR AND PUSHCHAIR ACCESS
Although the museum is underground and entered via steps, there is a lift
available on request. Once on site there is full access to all areas.

REFRESHMENTS
No.

SHOP
Small shop dedicated to war books and relevant wartime memorabilia.
Also jams, biscuits, pocket-money toys. Nothing exceptional for children.

TOILET FACILITIES
Wheelchair access. Baby-changing facilities in the ladies'.

CLOAKROOM
Supervised cloakroom.

PHOTOGRAPHY
Allowed and film sold.

DOGS
Guide dogs only.

THE CHILTERN OPEN-AIR MUSEUM

NEWLAND PARK, GORELANDS LANE, CHALFONT ST GILES, BUCKS, HP8 4AD
TEL: 01494 872163

HOW LONG SHOULD WE SPEND THERE?
Allow three to four hours.

WHICH AGE GROUP WILL IT APPEAL TO?
Over-eights will appreciate the educational side but younger children can run around and will enjoy the animals and nature trail.

INTRODUCTION
Rescued buildings are not the first thing that springs to mind when thinking of something to entertain children but two visits to this museum have proven a huge success.

The museum consists of 45 acres of parkland housing over 25 buildings of local historical interest and typical of the area. Under threat of demolition, these buildings have been moved to the museum and then carefully rebuilt. They include a 1950s telephone kiosk, a 1940s prefab, a barn dating back to 1595, work cottages dating back to the 1700s, and a toll house from the early 1800s. You roam through the parkland, stopping off at each of the buildings and examining the contents; the prefab, for example, is fitted out exactly as it would have been in the mid-1940s with typical utility furniture, electrical appliances and kitchen utensils all to be played with. We tried on period clothes and played with period toys in the Victorian Vicarage room and the farm workers' cottages were occupied by a couple in full costume who were happy to answer questions about the building, the people who would have lived there and the times in which they lived.

Outside in the park we stroked sheep and lambs and occasionally caught a glimpse of a horse and cart as it moved hay from the old barns. We completed the return journey via the all-natural play area and the park's nature trail, where we enjoyed spotting the nesting boxes, and recognised the trees and plants listed in the helpful leaflet bought from the shop. We finished off by exploring the Iron Age dwelling. One of the barns also houses an exhibition by The Hawk and Owl Trust – well worth allowing time for.

Due to the size of the site this is a very energetic day out and you must be prepared for quite a lot walking – definitely a fair weather activity.

HOW TO GET THERE AND WHERE TO PARK

Car: From the A413 at Chalfont St Giles and Chalfont St Peter follow the brown signs with the museum symbol. From the M25 take junction 17, Maple Cross and on the A412, follow the brown signs with the cart symbol. Parking is free and plentiful within the museum grounds.

OPENING HOURS

April to October, Saturday, Sunday and bank holidays,
11 a.m.–6 p.m.
April to October, Tuesday to Friday, 2 p.m.–6 p.m.
(In October the museum closes at 5 p.m. instead of 6 p.m.)
August: Tuesday to Sunday, 11 a.m.–6 p.m.
Car-park opens at 1 p.m. for picnics.

ADMISSION

Adults: £4. Children (5–16): £2.50. Under-fives: free. Senior citizens, unwaged, students and disabled: £3. Family ticket (two adults and two children): £12. Braille tapes and guides are available upon request.

WHEELCHAIR AND PUSHCHAIR ACCESS

Getting around the park on the track is no problem, although accessing some of the buildings can be a little tricky.

REFRESHMENTS

The cosy café is located at the far end of the park and serves delicious carrot cake at £1.25, tea at 80p and cans of drink for 75p. They also serve quiche, baked potatoes, sandwiches and soup with a roll. There is plenty of indoor seating with tasteful décor and the benches outside were surprisingly equipped with games such as wooden noughts and crosses. A bit cramped inside for pushchairs. We spotted just one high-chair and although eating your own food wouldn't be welcomed here the 'green' car-park adjacent to fields filled with horses is not an unpleasant spot for a picnic.

SHOP
The idiosyncratic little shop is also located at the far end of the park by the café and sells home-made jam and chutney, second-hand books and small inexpensive gifts, with all funds going to the upkeep of the museum. The nature trail leaflet costs 50p.

TOILET FACILITIES
These are located as you enter the park in a 1906 public convenience building with all original fittings! Wheelchair access is fine and there is a table in the ladies' that could be used for baby-changing – a bit draughty though! There are more toilets near the café at the far end of the park, located in a granary. There is a baby-changing area in the ladies' and disabled access in both the men's and ladies' which are reached by a ramp.

CLOAKROOM
No.

PHOTOGRAPHY
Allowed but no film sold.

DOGS
Allowed on leads but not welcome in the café.

THE DESIGN
MUSEUM

SHAD THAMES, LONDON, SE1 2YD
TEL: 0171 378 6055   FAX: 0171 378 6540

HOW LONG SHOULD WE SPEND THERE?
Allow about one hour.

WHICH AGE GROUP WILL IT APPEAL TO?
Suitable for over-eights.

INTRODUCTION
This is a very sophisticated museum best appreciated by older children. The ground floor is taken up by the shop, café and ticket office while the upper two floors are devoted to the exhibits.

The first floor Review Gallery is used for special temporary exhibitions and at present houses an exhibition of cycle design from 1825 to 2000 – from the primitive pedal-less hobby-horse bicycles through to futuristic mountain- and racing-bikes. The emphasis really is on cycle design rather than any complete history of bicycles as a means of transport and is, if possible, actually the more interesting for it as far as the kids were concerned since there are some very weird and wonderful machines on show. The only interactive element in the museum is currently to be found on this floor – a pair of exercise bikes attached to computerised monitoring equipment and with wall-mounted visual displays showing time, distance and speed – there are staff on hand to assist and explain and the children were encouraged to have a go on them.

From April 1998 this gallery will display an exhibition dedicated to Ferdinand Porsche and will feature the innovation and technology of

Porsche car design from 1900 to the present day.

The top floor houses the Collections Gallery which contains an eclectic selection of state-of-the-art designs for household items such as table lamps made from sand-blasted washing-machine door glass, beautifully streamlined ones and futuristic fridge/freezers. These complement small groups of themed classic exhibits on subjects such as one which had an educational approach to the the subject of plastics and the design of items which are in everyday use such as radios, packaging, telephones and household décor, that emphasise how – over the last century – design has become an integral part of functionality. Many of the exhibits on this floor are in glass cases but much of the very recent material is out in the open and it is rather intimidating to see these items surrounded with 'do not touch' notices – especially as many of them are almost too enticing not to touch. This is a unique specialised museum containing a wealth of beautiful exhibits but in truth it does have the air of a shrine to design and with its reverential quiet it struggles to hold the attention of children. To be fair it is not aimed specifically at children but we feel that although it barely merits inclusion as a full day's visit it is sufficiently interesting to older children to be worth a look – particularly if you combine it with one of the many other attractions in the vicinity.

HOW TO GET THERE AND WHERE TO PARK

Car: Park in the car- and coach-park at the Tower Bridge end of Tooley Street then it is about a five-minute walk or there is on-street meter parking in the immediate vicinity of the museum. A car-park is currently under construction opposite the museum.

Underground: A ten-minute walk from Tower Hill station (Circle and District lines) across Tower Bridge. Alternatively about a 20-minute walk from London Bridge station (Northern line) along the riverside walkway.

Train: Take the Docklands Light Railway to Tower Gateway station then a ten-minute walk across Tower Bridge. The nearest mainline station is London Bridge.

Boat: There is a regular service at weekends between 11 a.m. and 5 p.m. from Tower pier to London Bridge city or Butlers Wharf.

OPENING HOURS

All year, Monday to Friday, 11.30 a.m.–6 p.m.
Saturday and Sunday, 12–6 p.m.

ADMISSION

Adults: £5. Children (under 18): £3.75. Disabled visitors with a companion, students and registered unemployed: £3.75. Family ticket (two adults and two children): £12.

WHEELCHAIR AND PUSHCHAIR ACCESS

Full access throughout the museum with a lift to the upper floors and lots of space for wheels to manoeuvre in.

REFRESHMENTS

A splendid but expensive café looking out on the Thames. Sandwiches such as Red Leicester cheese on black rye or humus on sunflower and granary are £2.50. Soup and bread is affordable at £2 and their more substantial savouries include tarte provençale or chicken, ham and broccoli pie. There is a scrumptious range of cakes starting from 90p. No high-chairs were visible.

In the same building there is also a more formal restaurant called the Blue Print Cafe; this can be found around the front of the museum. It has spectacular views over the river and spectacular prices to go with it! Soup at £4.75, squid-ink tagliatelle at £5.50, spiced breast of chicken with lentils and yoghurt at £13.50 and sea bass with spinach in a white wine sauce at £16. A picnic is cheaper and if the weather is fine the riverside benches make a great spot for outdoor eating.

SHOP

A huge array of books on art and design and, as you might expect, a wonderful selection of beautifully designed items from watches and champagne glasses to household items of every shape, colour and function. In keeping with the quality of the merchandise the prices are on the high side – although many are surprisingly affordable and very difficult to resist. There is not a great deal in the way of items for children.

TOILET FACILITIES

Wheelchair-access and specially adapted toilets are available and there are baby-changing facilities.

CLOAKROOM

Supervised cloakroom available.

PHOTOGRAPHY
Allowed throughout the museum for private use only.

DOGS
Guide dogs only.

DIDCOT RAILWAY CENTRE

DIDCOT, OXFORDSHIRE, OX11 7NJ
TEL: 01235 817200

HOW LONG SHOULD WE SPEND THERE?
Allow one and a half hours.

WHICH AGE GROUP WILL IT APPEAL TO?
Suitable for all ages.

INTRODUCTION
Although I think that railway centres are only really fully appreciated by true enthusiasts (and the Didcot visitors' book attests to this), trains do have an enormous fascination for all small children. Situated on an unprepossessing site behind the modern Didcot station and in the shadow of a large power station, the centre aims to recapture some of the age of the Great Western Railway which ran until 1892. There is a collection of old engines in the engine shed – some of which can be boarded – which give a real feel for what it must have been like to stand on the footplate and stoke the boiler. On steam days you can ride on a train pulled by a 1930s steam engine on the main line and also on a branch line. Both are slightly disappointing in their brevity (although you could stay on board for endless repeat trips), but the branch-line train is beautifully restored. You can see engines being turned on the turntable, coaled and watered and how mailbags were exchanged at high speed. There is a lot of activity with buildings and trains being restored but this appeals mainly to the true aficionado.

Located in one of the platform buildings is a room which houses bygone relics such as restored name-plates, models, maps, tickets and period photos. There is also a display of original 1927 menus when lunch was still called luncheon and you could order roast mutton and onion sauce for three shillings (15p) and where you could fully expect to eat with silver-plated lobster picks and drink from GWR crockery. It all evokes an era of style and dignity long since lost.

HOW TO GET THERE AND WHERE TO PARK

Car: Signposted from A34 and easily reached from M40 junction 13. Free parking behind Julian's Garage opposite the station or in the market car-park.

Train: Didcot station on main line from London Paddington to Swindon.

OPENING HOURS

15 to 23 February, 28 March to 28 September, 25 October to 2 November and 27 December to 4 January, 10 a.m.–5 p.m.

November to February, 10 a.m.–4 p.m. (last admission 30 minutes before closing time).

ADMISSION

Steam days: Adults: £5. Children (over five): £3. Family ticket (two adults and two children): £14.50.

Static days: Adults: £3. Children (over five): £2. Family ticket (two adults and two children): £9.50.

Santa days: £5.50 for everyone.

Prices for special events on request.

WHEELCHAIR AND PUSHCHAIR ACCESS

No easy access for wheels. If you can negotiate the steep flights of steps beyond the entrance tunnel the ground is pretty flat, but wheelchair users could not access the steam-train rides or the engine shed – both of which are the main attraction.

REFRESHMENTS

Rather basic café with limited seating but lots of space. Tea 60p, cappuccino 85p, small range of sandwiches, cakes, scones, doughnuts, sweets and crisps. No high-chairs. You may prefer the benches outside and there is a picnic area between the engine shed and the main line; not as grim as it sounds since it's dotted with fruit trees but you'll be accompanied by the relentless noise of the steam train chugging up and down.

SHOP

A railway lover's paradise with plenty of Thomas the Tank Engine merchandise for the kids; videos, postcards, posters and specialised railway books for anoraks!

TOILET FACILITIES

Baby-changing facilities and wheelchair-access toilet are one and the same. Ladies' toilet has a child-height seat.

CLOAKROOM

No.

PHOTOGRAPHY

Allowed.

DOGS

Allowed, if kept on a lead.

DUXFORD AIRFIELD

DUXFORD, CAMBRIDGESHIRE, CB2 4QR
TEL: 01223 835000/0891 516816 (EVENTS HOTLINE)

HOW LONG SHOULD WE SPEND THERE?
Allow four hours.

WHICH AGE GROUP WILL IT APPEAL TO?
Suitable for over-fives.

INTRODUCTION
Duxford used to be an operational RAF airfield and, although there are a lot of static exhibits here, it's best to visit during one of the air shows to get the most out of the day. The air shows vary slightly, depending on the theme that has been chosen, however they usually feature historic fighting aircraft and – if you're lucky – the Red Arrows. A leaflet is published each year outlining the programme. Even for the uninitiated the adrenalin-rush that comes from the proximity to a Tornado F3 as it slices through the sky just in front of you at deafening noise levels is astonishing. Be warned, small children may find the noise too much. Such raw power contrasts with the grace and skill of the biplane aerobatics team whose dazzling routines as they come within a hair's breadth of each other are breathtaking. There is also a fine mix of excitement and nostalgia at seeing older fighting aircraft such as Spitfires and Messerschmitts dog-fighting above you. There's a friendly atmosphere as veterans and children mingle to watch these historical aircraft go through their paces.

You should also try to visit the 140 historic aircraft spread around the various hangars on the site, including the new American Air Museum. For a small, extra charge you can go on board an old Concorde and other airliners. You can buy a programme, but the information tent which is set up on display days will tell you what's happening when. There's an outdoor playground and an indoor interactive play area which is themed around aerodynamics and aircraft construction – not as dull as it sounds – where you can mount a stationary bicycle and, by peddling like crazy, power a large aircraft propeller to spin the rider around in a circle – definitely worth a visit.

HOW TO GET THERE AND WHERE TO PARK
Car: Eight miles south of Cambridge next to junction 10 of the M11. Also easily accessible from A1 and M1. Masses of free car-parking on site.

OPENING HOURS
Mid-March to mid-October, daily, 10 a.m.–6 p.m.
Mid-October to mid-March, daily, 10 a.m.–4 p.m.

ADMISSION
Adults: £6.40. Children (5–15): £3.20. Students and unemployed: £3.20. Under-fives: free. Family ticket (two adults and up to three children): £18. Disabled visitors and carers: half–price.

WHEELCHAIR AND PUSHCHAIR ACCESS
Very good: fully accessible site – although it is not always possible to board and view the aircraft.

REFRESHMENTS
There is a restaurant and a café serving basic hot and cold food. High-chairs available. During an airshow there are various stalls selling everything from fish and chips to freshly made doughnuts.

SHOP
During an airshow a large part of the site is devoted to an array of stalls selling plane-related merchandise from model kits to flight jackets.

TOILET FACILITIES
Wheelchair access and baby-changing facilities are available near the café.

CLOAKROOM
No.

EPPING FOREST

EPPING FOREST INFORMATION CENTRE, HIGH BEACH, LOUGHTON, ESSEX
TEL: 0181 508 0028   FAX: 0181 532 0188

HOW LONG SHOULD WE SPEND THERE?
Allow two hours to a whole day.

WHICH AGE GROUP WILL IT APPEAL TO?
Suitable for all ages.

INTRODUCTION
It's easy to forget that there is this 6,000-acre expanse of ancient woodland on the edge of north-east London which provides a wonderful free day out and a refreshing antidote to inner-city life. As the forest extends over a ten-mile-long crescent it is accessible from a variety of places and by many different means of transport.

The information centre at High Beach provides an ideal focal point for a visit and you can either park in the small car-park there or by the King's Oak pub in Nursery Road. The pub will not do anything to promote an image of rural retreat since it is the meeting place of mobile Essex youth and the surrounding roads can be made quite terrifying by speeding cars and bikes. Don't be put off, though, as they don't stray far and it's easy to escape this; you're not far into the forest before the traffic noise becomes a distant hum drowned out by birds and the wind. You can walk for miles along designated paths, and a visit to the information centre before you set off will be helpful as they sell modestly priced brochures and leaflets outlining different walks and the friendly, knowledgeable staff will advise you on anything specific you want to know. The forest is rich in wildlife and at the information centre there's usually a display of flora and fauna to look out for according to the season and also a quick check-list on a blackboard outside the centre. Still, there are always surprises if you keep your eyes and ears open; such as the adder we saw slithering away; the bright orange fungi; the sound of woodpeckers or even a glimpse of the deer which still roam freely. Despite the paths being laid with wood bark in many places, it can get muddy – especially where the path serves as a bridleway – so wear sturdy footwear.

HOW TO GET THERE AND WHERE TO PARK

Car: Take junction 26 off M25. The information centre is signposted off the roundabout at this junction. Follow Skillet Hill road and don't miss the right-hand turn down a lane called Forestside – just past a pub on the right – towards the sign for the youth hostel (the information centre is not signposted here and if you miss it it's a long journey round).

Underground: Around a ten-minute walk into the forest from either Theydon Bois or Loughton stations.

Train: From Liverpool Street to Chingford station and then a ten-minute walk into the forest.

The information centre can only be reached by car or taxi from one of the above stations.

OPENING HOURS

The forest is not enclosed so there is year-round access.

The information centre is open as follows:

1 April to 31 October, Monday to Saturday, 10 a.m.–5 p.m. Sunday 11 a.m.–5 p.m.

1 November to 31 March, Monday to Friday, 2 p.m.–5 p.m. (or dusk if earlier), Saturday 10 a.m.–5 p.m. (or dusk) and Sunday 11 a.m.–5 p.m. (or dusk).

Closed: 24 December–2 January.

ADMISSION

Free.

WHEELCHAIR AND PUSHCHAIR ACCESS

Pushchair access is good if you don't mind a bit of mud or tracks that are less than pavement-smooth. Wheelchair users are advised to use the paths recommended by the information centre.

REFRESHMENTS

The King's Oak claims to serve a wide variety of food although we have not tried it. There's also a refreshment hut next to the pub serving ice-cream, sweets and hot-dog and burger-type fare. There are plenty of other pubs in the area, and the occasional refreshment hut within the forest. In our opinion, however, you can't beat a picnic in the heart of the forest.

SHOP
The information centre sells a very small range of pocket-money toys, greetings cards and leaflets about the forest.

TOILET FACILITIES
Wheelchair-access toilets in the information centre but no baby-changing facilities.

CLOAKROOM
No.

PHOTOGRAPHY
Allowed.

DOGS
Allowed.

GEFFRYE MUSEUM

KINGSLAND ROAD, LONDON, E2 8EA
TEL: 0171 739 9893/0171 739 8543 (RECORDED INFORMATION)
FAX: 0171 729 5647

HOW LONG SHOULD WE SPEND THERE?
Allow one and a half hours.

WHICH AGE GROUP WILL IT APPEAL TO?
Suitable for over-eights.

INTRODUCTION
The museum is housed in Ironmongers' Company almshouses which date from the 1740s and are set amongst attractive gardens. It was an important centre for furniture-making from the 1880s onwards. The museum now consists of 14 converted houses and a meeting room and it opened as a museum in 1914 – the time when the area was the centre of the East End furniture trade. It presents the changing styles of house interiors from the 1600s to post-war years. The rooms are beautifully authentic but the attention of our small children was not held for very long. Although the museum has a timetable of workshops for children (listed in the leaflet available at the ticket kiosk), we felt it was the older child who would benefit more from this popular and unusual venue. The museum has recently received a lottery grant and from autumn 1998 will double in size with new galleries and restaurant facilities and full wheelchair accessibility.

HOW TO GET THERE AND WHERE TO PARK
Car: Limited parking available in neighbouring streets and on Sundays parking is easier as you can park on single yellow lines.
Underground: Liverpool Street station then take the bus – 22A, 22B or 149

– from Bishopsgate. Old Street station (exit 2) then 15 minutes' walk or bus 243.
Train: Dalston Kingsland or Liverpool Street stations.

OPENING HOURS

All year, Tuesday to Saturday, 10 a.m.–5 p.m. Sundays and bank holiday Mondays 2 p.m.–5 p.m.
Closed: Monday (except bank holidays), 1 January, Good Friday, 24–26 December.
Walled herb garden open April to October during museum opening hours.

ADMISSION

Free.

WHEELCHAIR AND PUSHCHAIR ACCESS

Special facilities for disabled visitors. Access for wheels is good although the café is narrow and manoeuvrability difficult. There is only stair access to the second floor although at the time of writing this had just one decorated room.

REFRESHMENTS

The small café located halfway through the museum building on the ground floor is pleasant although the staff were rather brusque. Coffee sold at 90p, tea at 60p, orange and apple juice at 50p. There is no hot food but cakes such as banana and chocolate fudge are 75p to £1.40. No high-chairs. The garden has plenty of benches for picnics.

SHOP

Plenty of pocket-money toys, toiletries, tea towels, postcards. There is a small section especially for kids with quiz sheets at 5p. There is also a good selection of books on art and design, gardening and furniture.

TOILET FACILITIES

At the south end of the building where you enter although you will have to negotiate two small steps. There are no baby-changing facilities in either the north or south end toilets and the north end is not accessible to wheelchairs or pushchairs.

CLOAKROOM

Available.

PHOTOGRAPHY
Allowed but no film sold.

DOGS
Guide dogs only.

THE GLOBE THEATRE

NEW GLOBE WALK, SOUTHWARK, LONDON, SE1 9DR
TEL: 0171 902 1500   FAX: 0171 902 1515

HOW LONG SHOULD WE SPEND THERE?
Allow about one and a half hours.

WHICH AGE GROUP WILL IT APPEAL TO?
Suitable for over-fives.

INTRODUCTION
The Globe is not one of the cheaper outings there is, but it is so unique that it just has to be included. The site is still under development inasmuch as there are plans to build an indoor theatre (the Inigo Jones Theatre) with a full-scale exhibition, conference centre, library and cinema beneath it. Funds for this are not yet available and so in the meantime the small exhibition partially occupies this site. This consists of a number of information boards, models and a video about the research involved in reconstructing the theatre and a little of the history of London in Elizabethan times. There is a strong emphasis on the skills employed to complete the Herculean task of rebuilding the Globe in faithful and minute detail and this, now finished and having completed its first full season in summer 1997, is truly splendid.

The highlight of the visit is undoubtedly the hour-long tour where the expert guides, exuding pride, describe the construction of the building – details such as how it took two years to find the right oak trees to make the two pillars at the front of the stage and how every oak balustrade in the balconies was hand-carved by one woman using a hand lathe. The guides also succeed in evoking the atmosphere of the unique performances where, amongst other features, 500 people – groundlings – can stand in the pit at the foot of the stage, moving around and heckling as they see fit. It is hard to believe that a visit such as this would appeal to kids reared on computer games but so attractive was this experience made to sound that our nine- and seven-year-olds were prompted to ask if they could go and sit through a three- to four-hour performance during the play season in the summer; a testimony as much to the skills of our guide as to the wondrous site itself.

HOW TO GET THERE AND WHERE TO PARK

Car: There is a car-park at the Tower Bridge end of Tooley Street after Morgans Lane which, while reasonably priced, is a 30-minute walk along the riverbank from the theatre. Parking is free at weekends on the meters in adjacent streets.

Underground: A ten-minute walk from London Bridge station (Northern line).

Train: A ten-minute walk from London Bridge station or alternatively Cannon Street or Blackfriars stations on the north side of the river which can be crossed by either Southwark or Blackfriars bridges, it's about a 20-minute walk from either of these though.

OPENING HOURS

May to September (play season), 9 a.m.–12.15 p.m. and 2 p.m.–4 p.m. (Access is limited during this period.)
October to April, 10 a.m.–5 p.m.

ADMISSION

Adults: £5. Children (under-15): £3. Senior citizens and students: £4. Family ticket (two adults and up to three children): £14.

WHEELCHAIR AND PUSHCHAIR ACCESS

Wide open spaces are easily negotiable by wheelchair or pushchair with lifts to the upper floors.

REFRESHMENTS

The Globe Café is modern and spacious with wonderful views over the Thames to the floodlit St Paul's which looks truly spectacular at night. Try a Globe cream tea for £4.75. Either of the warm apple and cinnamon or feta and sundried tomato scones at £1.60 is delicious. Only one sandwich choice – mature Cheddar cheese and apple chutney in a cracked wheat roll at £2.95 with the scrumptious cakes from £1 to £2.75 and tempting desserts – resist if you can hot toffee and banana sundae or chocolate bread-and-butter pudding with toasted hazelnut cream. The café is open from 10 a.m. to last orders at 11 p.m. The other alternative is the Globe Restaurant which, as the name suggests, is altogether more formal and serves more substantial meals. Main courses start at £8.50 and there are set two- and three-course menus. The restaurant is open for lunch from 12 noon to 2.30 p.m. and for dinner from 5.30 p.m. to last orders at 11 p.m.; there is also a pre-theatre menu available during the play season. Both the café and the restaurant are licensed and reservations are recommended for the restaurant.

SHOP
The shop is quite expensive, and sells editions of all of Shakespeare's plays, prints of London, T-shirts, sweatshirts, 'Elizabethan' preserves and an unusual selection of items made from the oak wood used to build the theatre such as buttons, light pulls and ornaments. Open from 10 a.m. to 5 p.m.

TOILET FACILITIES
Full wheelchair-access toilet but no baby-changing facilities.

CLOAKROOM
No.

PHOTOGRAPHY
Allowed during the tours but not during the actual performances.

DOGS
Guide dogs only.

HAMPTON COURT PALACE

EAST MOLESEY, SURREY, KT8 9AU
TEL: 0181 781 9500

HOW LONG SHOULD WE SPEND THERE?
Allow four hours.

WHICH AGE GROUP WILL IT APPEAL TO?
Suitable for all ages.

INTRODUCTION
A very appropriate destination for when the children start to study the
Tudors at school but also a great day out at any time. In fact not much
remains of the original Tudor palace built for Cardinal Wolsey and taken
over by Henry VIII, the building having been substantially altered over
several centuries of royal occupancy. The Tudor Great Hall is magnificent
and the kitchens, apparently the most extensive surviving 16th-century
kitchens in Europe, are fascinating. Here you will find stuffed boar and
peacock ready to be served at a typical royal banquet, roaring fires in huge
hearths and the smell of fresh herbs. The Baroque King's and Queen's
apartments are in fact those of William III and Mary and the King's
apartments now show no signs of the devastating damage inflicted by the
terrible fire of 1986 thanks to their skilled restoration.

There are six routes to follow around the Palace and these are all
signposted from the Clock Court. Additionally, the information centre was
happy to provide free family trail sheets for the Tudor kitchens and the
King's apartments; similar trails were advertised for the Georgian rooms
but none were available. Also, they supply recorded tours and it is here
that you can book guided tours. The guidebook is £3.95 but the very

friendly staff are also pleased to help with information. The family ticket entitled you to entry to the gardens too where smaller children can let off steam and grown-ups can admire the truly beautiful formal gardens and the great vine (with its alcoholic by-products). Horse-drawn carriage rides leave from the east front entrance for £13 per carriage (Monday 10.15 a.m. to 5.30 p.m. and all other days 9.30 a.m. to 5.30 p.m.). If you feel like going further afield the park grounds extend over 60 acres but even if you don't manage to fully explore them the one 'must' on the itinerary is the world-renowned Maze (adults £2.20 and children £1.50 if not pre-paid).

HOW TO GET THERE AND WHERE TO PARK

Car: Follow signs for Kingston-upon-Thames. Palace located off the A508. Free car-parking on Hampton Court Green opposite the Palace. Parking also available inside the Palace grounds at £2.

Train: Direct line from Waterloo to Hampton Court station, the journey taking 30 minutes approximately. Then a ten-minute walk from the station to the Palace.

Boat: Summer only. Three-hour journey from Westminster pier.

OPENING HOURS

Mid-October to mid-April, Mondays, 10.15 a.m.–4.30 p.m. Tuesdays to Sundays 9.30 a.m.–4.30 p.m. (Last admission 3.45 p.m.) Mid-April to mid-October, Mondays 10.15 a.m.–6 p.m. Tuesdays to Sundays 9.30 a.m.–6 p.m. (Last admission 5.15 p.m.)
Closed: 24–26 December.

ADMISSION

Adults: £8.50. Children (5–15): £5.60. Senior citizens and students: £6.50. Family ticket (two adults plus two or three children or one adult plus up to four children): £25.40. Under-fives: free. The tickets allow access to the Palace, gardens and maze.

WHEELCHAIR AND PUSHCHAIR ACCESS

Ramps are provided in most cases but some entrances and exits can only be accessed by stairs. A lift, however, can be used to access almost all of the Palace and the flat gardens are easily negotiated; wardens are happy to help on request. Only the Wolsey Rooms are completely inaccessible. Battery-powered cars are available free of charge for use in the gardens.

REFRESHMENTS

The Tiltyard Tea Room in the gardens behind the ticket office serves very acceptable fare in a light spacious area with a terrace outside. Ciabatta with brie and pesto £2.55, cakes from £1.95, children's pick 'n' mix boxes with healthy options, sandwiches from £2.20, chicken and broccoli with pepper sauce or sweet and sour pork £5.20, home-made carrot and coriander soup with roll £2.20, tea 90p, coffee pot £1, soft drinks from 95p. There is a coffee shop (Privy Kitchen) in the Palace which is open from 10 a.m.–5 p.m. serving light dishes and there are ice-cream kiosks. For picnics you can head for the Wilderness area in the grounds outside the Tiltyard Tea Room but picnics are not permitted elsewhere.

SHOP
There are several shops but they all share the same up-market good taste on the whole, with glassware, jams, chutneys, pewter, cards, toiletries, historical books and confectionery. They don't all have quite the same merchandise; the Tudor Kitchen shop for example has a strong culinary theme with a wide range of herbs and kitchen utensils. They all sell pocket-money toys too.

TOILET FACILITIES
All have wheelchair access but, bizarrely, the tea-room toilets have the baby-changing facilities inside one of just four regular toilet booths so you can imagine the queues and the frustration if you have a screaming baby.

CLOAKROOM
Not available.

PHOTOGRAPHY
Not allowed in many of the Palace rooms but permitted elsewhere. Film sold.

DOGS
Guide dogs only.

HATFIELD HOUSE
AND GARDENS

HATFIELD, HERTFORDSHIRE, AL9 5NQ
TEL: 01707 262823/265159

HOW LONG SHOULD WE SPEND THERE?
Allow one hour for the house and three hours to a full day if you include the gardens.

WHICH AGE GROUP WILL IT APPEAL TO?
Suitable for all ages.

INTRODUCTION
This beautiful Jacobean house, set in its own extensive grounds on north London's doorstep, is a source of delight. Regrettably there is no children's quiz for the house but our kids still enjoyed the hour's wander. You can always find plenty of details to interest them amongst the rich contents of the house which reveal its strong links with Elizabeth I who spent much of her childhood here – although the original remaining wing of the Royal Palace of Hatfield is not open to the public (other than for the regular Elizabethan banquets). The wonderful formal gardens are full of surprises with little fountains and quiet benches tucked around secret corners. On the lawn outside the old palace a band played and the scent of crushed lavender filled the air. You can continue into the wilder gardens which are full of daffodils in the spring and where the children can run, hide and generally enjoy the wonderful surroundings. The park itself, on the far side of the house, offers a well-planned play area and wooden equipment with masses of space and organised trails (leaflets available). There is a house guidebook available at £1.70. Carriage rides start from outside the garden shop and cost £1.50 for kids and £2 for adults. Don't miss the

exhibition of model soldiers in the stable block; although very static the sheer number – over 3,000 – is remarkable.

HOW TO GET THERE AND WHERE TO PARK
Car: Signposted off Junction 4 of the A1 or easy access from the M1. Plenty of free parking inside the grounds.

Train: Hatfield railway station is directly opposite the main entrance so it couldn't be more convenient; but if you attempt this route with a pushchair beware – the station is not wheels-friendly with a hideous footbridge to negotiate. Mainline from King's Cross takes 23 minutes.

OPENING HOURS
House: 25 March to 12 October, Monday to Saturday, 12 noon for guided tours only. Last tour 4 p.m. Sundays 1 p.m.–4.30 p.m. No guided tours available. (Also open Easter weekend, May Day, Spring and August bank holiday Mondays 11 a.m.–4.30 p.m. but no guided tours available.)
Closed: Monday. Good Friday.
Park: 25 March to 12 October, daily, 10.30 a.m.–8 p.m. daily (except Good Friday). Last entry 5 p.m.
West Garden: 25 March to 12 October, daily (except Good Friday), 11 a.m.–6 p.m.
East Garden: 25 March to 12 October, Mondays only (except bank holidays), 2 p.m.–5 p.m.

ADMISSION
Adults: £5.70. Children (5–16): £3.40. Senior citizens: £4.80. Under-fives: free. No family ticket available. Prices include entrance to the house, park and gardens.

WHEELCHAIR AND PUSHCHAIR ACCESS
There are steep steps at the front of the house but wheelchairs can gain access by a separate door on request at the entrance. There is a lift to the upper floor and the attendants will be pleased to assist you. All the small flights of steps within the house have ramps. There is no access to the model soldiers exhibition for wheels.

REFRESHMENTS
A pleasant, bright and spacious self-service restaurant can be found in the stable block. We spotted two high-chairs. Food was reasonably priced and not bad in terms of price and quality with home-made soup and a roll at £2, Welsh rarebit £2, baked potato from £1.90 – with an exciting range of

fillings on offer, sandwiches at £1.85 and gourmet baguettes at £2.85. Coffee 85p, pot of tea 90p, minerals 85p, fresh orange juice £1.10. There are also several tables and benches outside in a sheltered courtyard, but for picnics head for the wide open spaces of the park where there are benches and tables dotted around including an area overlooking the play area; or simply drop your blanket wherever – there are no restrictions other than in the formal garden.

SHOP
There is a garden shop which is well stocked with plants and bushes and two gift shops. The stable shop has a wide range of merchandise including some more imaginative pocket-money toys for kids, such as books, puzzles and a plethora of gift items. The Still Room is rather more expensive and has more breakables, so beware with toddlers, but worth a look for toiletries, candles and range of mustards and pickles.

TOILET FACILITIES
Spartan baby room and separate toilet with wheelchair access.

CLOAKROOM
No

PHOTOGRAPHY
No photography allowed in the house.

DOGS
Allowed in the park but guide dogs only in the house.

HOLLAND PARK

▲▲▲

KENSINGTON HIGH STREET, LONDON, W8
TEL: 0171 602 2226

HOW LONG SHOULD WE SPEND THERE?
Allow about one and a half hours.

WHICH AGE GROUP WILL IT APPEAL TO?
Suitable for all ages.

INTRODUCTION
Another true gem of a city park – a real retreat from the urban chaos of
the surrounding streets. A highlight for children is the large supervised
adventure play area packed with slides, wooden towers, bridges, rope
swings and other challenging activities for the over-fives with a booking
system for the small-scale softball tennis. There is also a rather less
daunting play area for younger children; both are open from 10 a.m. to 6
p.m., seven days a week. There are tables and benches next to the play
area, some of which are under cover, making it an ideal spot for a picnic
or simply reading the paper while keeping an eye on the children. There
is also an area for toddlers beyond the Orangery and close to the café
with seats and benches there too. Amongst the buildings in the centre of
the park is an ecological centre open for groups and advance bookings
only. There is a beautiful, tranquil Japanese garden, sections of formal
garden, the Orangery which is used for a variety of purposes (a local
school was performing a carol concert there on the afternoon we visited)
and something called the Ice House, which is used for displays and
exhibitions. There's a mass of space to run around in if you can prise the
kids away from the adventure play area but bikes are not allowed in the
park. For the sports-minded there are tennis courts and a bowling green.

HOW TO GET THERE AND WHERE TO PARK

Car: Approach via Holland Park Avenue and then turn down Holland Park
(the road running alongside the park itself). There is a small car-park
or there is plenty of on-street parking which is free on Sundays on
single yellow lines.

Underground: A five-minute walk from Holland Park station (Central
line).

Train: A ten-minute walk from Kensington Olympia station.

OPENING HOURS

All year, daily, 7 a.m.–dusk.

ADMISSION

Free.

WHEELCHAIR AND PUSHCHAIR ACCESS

Lots of wide open spaces and very few problems with access except to the
Japanese garden.

REFRESHMENTS

There are two options. One is the rather expensive Belvedere Restaurant
next to the Orangery where you can try the starters such as soup at £3.50,
grilled goats' cheese, radicchio and frisee salad at £6.10 and the main
courses that feature dishes such as chicken with Mediterranean
vegetables, polenta and rosemary oil and are priced between £9 and
£12.50. The Belvedere is open from Monday to Sunday from 12 noon to 3
p.m. for lunch and from Monday to Saturday from 7 p.m. to 11 p.m. for
dinner. There are various recommendations in the window including
Time Out and so although we didn't actually try it ourselves, we feel
confident about its inclusion. A less salubrious but nonetheless worthy
watering hole is the park café where the queue testified to its popularity.
There are lots of tables outside and limited seating inside with no high-
chairs. The menu includes cheese rolls with slabs of juicy beef tomatoes at
£1.20, baguette sandwiches at £1.40, home-made vegetable soup at £1.20
and other hot food including spaghetti bolognese at £3.20, chilli and
baked potatoes from £1.30, all of which were well made and came in
hearty portions. There is a small range of delicious cakes, such as plum
tart, from £1; tea is 40p and coffee is 55p.

SHOP

No.

TOILET FACILITIES
There are public toilets in the centre of the park with a family room which has baby-changing facilities and a separate wheelchair-access toilet which is kept locked.

CLOAKROOM
No.

PHOTOGRAPHY
Allowed throughout the park.

DOGS
Allowed if kept on a lead.

HOUSE ON THE HILL
TOY MUSEUM

STANSTED, ESSEX, CM24 8SP
TEL: 01279 813237/0891 424103 (24-HOUR INFORMATION LINE)
FAX: 01279 816391

HOW LONG SHOULD WE SPEND THERE?
Allow one hour.

WHICH AGE GROUP WILL IT APPEAL TO?
Suitable for all ages.

INTRODUCTION
Large but not grand, with over 25,000 exhibits spread across two floors.
You may not choose this museum visit as the sole attraction, but if you're
at the castle anyway, it's worth a visit – although we found the place
somewhat soulless. There is an animated theatre show, prolific displays of
dolls, a Meccano fairground, a Peter Pan window and a German
battlefield manned by toy soldiers that can be lit up; although on the
whole the museum is not particularly interactive. The display cases with
Star Wars and space exhibits were interesting and there is a great train set
and Scalextric set. Pick up a worksheet at the shop to make the visit more
interesting.

HOW TO GET THERE AND WHERE TO PARK
Car: Exit at junction 8 off the M11 then follow signs for Mountfitchet
     Castle. Car-parking plentiful and free.
Train: Stansted Mountfitchet station, from Liverpool Street to Cambridge.
     Three minutes' walk from station.

OPENING HOURS
16 March to 12 November, daily 10 a.m.–5 p.m. (Last admission 4 p.m.)
Open every weekend all year.

ADMISSION
Adults: £3. Children (under-14): £2.20. Senior citizens and students: £2.60.
Infants: free.

WHEELCHAIR AND PUSHCHAIR ACCESS
A very steep approach to the museum, with the exhibits arranged on two
floors, also there is no lift, which makes access to the second floor very
difficult.

REFRESHMENTS
No catering facilities at all, although there is a small school-room where
you could have a picnic. You could eat at the Mountfitchet Castle café but
you would have to pay to get in. There are several tea rooms and cafés on
the high street.

SHOP
An interesting, reasonably sized shop located at the entrance/exit with
genuine collector's items on sale and more modestly priced notepads and
pencils for £1.50. Worksheets are on sale for 20p. Not very inspiring but
better than the shop at the castle.

TOILET FACILITIES
There are no wheelchair-access toilets or baby-changing facilities.

CLOAKROOM
No cloakroom.

PHOTOGRAPHY
Not allowed.

DOGS
Not allowed.

IMPERIAL WAR MUSEUM

LAMBETH ROAD, LONDON, SE1 6HZ
TEL: 0171 416 5320 (ENQUIRIES)/
0891 600 140 (RECORDED INFORMATION)

HOW LONG SHOULD WE SPEND THERE?
Allow four to five hours.

WHICH AGE GROUP WILL IT APPEAL TO?
Suitable for all ages.

INTRODUCTION
We went to this museum with some trepidation as I had really expected some dour and sabre-rattling affair. I was very wrong; it made a great day out and the museum's awards for Museum of the Year and Building of the Year in 1990 are well deserved. There are a great many exhibits to see from the ground floor, with its array of tanks, rockets, auxiliary vehicles, artillery and planes suspended from the ceiling. The lower ground floor is packed with exhibits primarily from the two world wars through to the Gulf, and is enlivened by archive film on video. There are also telephone tapes, where you can listen to real-life experiences. You can walk through the dark and noisy Trench Experience – complete with authentic smells – with models talking you through cameos of life in trench warfare; or you can be taken through the imaginative Blitz Experience complete with moving floors to simulate the bomb strikes. The queues for this were long (although we waited only 20 minutes), but if we'd known, we'd have headed for this as soon as we arrived. Both of these could be a bit too terrifying for toddlers or sensitive older children, as could the small room devoted to Belsen. The galleries are well laid out and packed with clear and

71

informative exhibits relating to different aspects of both world wars and many campaigns, as well as showing life on the home front and the cultural changes each war engendered.

The first floor holds more heavy hardware and a fascinating permanent exhibition called Secret War about espionage and intelligence-gathering by special agents during both world wars, touching on its relevance to modern day. The second floor is dedicated to art galleries.

At the time of visiting development was under way to create new exhibitions dedicated to the Holocaust and Total War scheduled to be finished in 2000. Try and catch the free films and gallery talks.

A guidebook for £2.50 is sold at the ticket kiosk and a free leaflet listing current and forthcoming exhibitions with a separate floorplan is available from the reception. Touch-screen databases are dotted around and although you are not allowed to touch or climb on the vehicles there was plenty to keep most ages happy.

HOW TO GET THERE AND WHERE TO PARK

Car: There is no designated car-park and parking is restricted in the surrounding roads to meter and pay-and-display spaces. Sundays are a little easier when there are spaces on Lambeth Road on single yellow lines.

Underground: Twenty minutes' walk from either Waterloo or Elephant and Castle stations.

Train: Twenty minutes' walk from Waterloo station.

Bus: Numbers: 1, 3, 12, 45, 53, 63, 159, 168, 171.

OPENING HOURS

Open all year, daily, 10 a.m.–6 p.m.
Closed: 24–26 December.

ADMISSION

Adults: £4.70. Children (5–16): £2.35. Senior citizens, students and registered unemployed: £3.70. Family ticket (two adults and up to four children): £12.50. *Disabled visitors*: Adults: £2.35. Senior citizens and registered unemployed: £1.85.Children: £1.15. The museum is free after 4.30 p.m.

WHEELCHAIR AND PUSHCHAIR ACCESS

The signs outside state fully accessible with the best entry to use being the west entrance (there are steep steps in the approach to the main entrance and a short flight of steps into the ground floor exhibition area). There is a lift to all floors at the back of the museum, but this is not clearly signposted if you enter from the front.

REFRESHMENTS

A truly excellent self-service licensed café located on the ground floor boasts one of the most imaginative menus we have found at a museum venue. The surroundings are pleasantly cool with a light, bright atmosphere and fresh flowers on the tables. There is plenty of room for pushchairs and wheelchairs – except, perhaps, on the busiest days – but surprisingly only one high-chair was available.

Choose from a hot or cold menu of spring vegetable pasta bake with wine at £5.25, home-made soup with baguette or exotic salads. No boring cheese and tomato sandwiches here but take your pick from goats' cheese and roast pepper baguette at £2.65, humus and salad in a sunflower bap at £2.25 and less exotic sandwiches from £1.95. There is an excellent morning coffee and afternoon tea menu served all day with a selection of home-made cakes from £1.75, tea at 95p a pot and both filter coffee and cappuccino at £1.10. The children's menu was surprisingly disappointing with the usual fare of sausage and mash with fizzy drink and chocolate crispy cake for £2.75. No doubt it would have been beautifully cooked, but why is it always assumed that the lowest common denominator is the right choice for kids? A healthier alternative would have been welcome. Open until 5.30 p.m. daily with the lunch menu served from 12 noon–3 p.m.

Those with their own food can eat in the rather soulless 'picnic room' at the back of the museum (not signposted but the helpful attendant at the entrance told us about it on the way in) which is open at weekends and during school holidays only; this is clearly the schools' feeding chamber equipped with drinks and chocolate dispenser and drinking water.

Alternatively there is the large park surrounding the museum which makes for a more attractive venue in fine weather. There are several picnic tables and benches with a kiosk open every day from 10 a.m.–6.30 p.m.

SHOP

Very tasteful merchandise with reasonable space to move around. All carefully themed around war or fashion, given the Forties Fashion exhibition was on when we visited. Posters at £2.99, puzzles, kitsch lighters or cufflinks, mock period radiograms and pocket-money toys. All the spy and secret agent equipment, such as John Adams spy kits and Dorling Kindersley secret detective boxes, were much sought after by our nine-year-old.

TOILET FACILITIES
Pleasant baby-changing room with a separate toilet, playpen for toddlers and a screen should you want to breastfeed; unfortunately, it was down a small, steep flight of steps, although there is a lift which is not clearly signposted. Toilets with wheelchair access on all floors. The signs in this area could be much improved and until it is, I thoroughly recommend the floor plan obtainable at reception.

CLOAKROOM
Supervised cloakroom where they are happy to store buggies if needed.

PHOTOGRAPHY
Allowed (except in the special Forties Fashion room) and film sold at reception.

DOGS
Guide dogs only.

KEW BRIDGE
STEAM MUSEUM

GREEN DRAGON LANE, BRENTFORD, MIDDLESEX, TW8 0EN
TEL: 0181 568 4757

HOW LONG SHOULD WE SPEND THERE?
Allow two hours.

WHICH AGE GROUP WILL IT APPEAL TO?
Suitable for over-fives.

INTRODUCTION
Don't be put off by what you might consider the rather uninspiring subjects of water and steam engines. This treasure of a small museum is housed in the original nineteenth-century water-pumping station and has recently added a new gallery with the help of National Lottery funding and now offers excellent value for money. The new Water For Life gallery is as yet incomplete (awaiting further funding), but still manages to transform what used to be a remote technical experience into something much more accessible for children – we can state this with complete confidence having experienced both the 'before' and the 'after'. The theme of the gallery is the importance of water to London, how it has vitally affected the city's development from its Roman founding on a site close to a water source to important historical events such as the Plague and Great Fire of London. As you enter you can see the various types of water piping which have been used from Roman times – including the bored out elm wood tree trunks of the Georgian period – and as you step into the main hall you do so through a mocked-up section of the London Ring Main built in 1994 to solve London's modern-day water-supply problems.

Explanations are clear and not at all long-winded and there are Roman artefacts, drawers to pull out with additional, prolific information and excellent illustrations. Naturally the most fascinating parts for children are always the most gruesome, so the spyholes and cameras into imitation sewers revealing rats and the list of what horrors have been found in various sewers (including a crocodile in the labyrinthine tunnels beneath Paris) are big favourites. The underground lives of flushers and toshers also make interesting reading. There isn't a huge amount of interactivity but enough to make the experience more stimulating and, let's face it, it is quite a feat to turn the subject of water and sewers into something that you would want to interact with at all.

The next floor houses several smaller pumping engines all of which are operational. From here you get a good view of the enormous wall in the Water For Life gallery which is covered chronologically from floor to ceiling with vessels, machines and artefacts; a Victorian bath and shower, beautifully decorated toilet bowls, shiny boilers, a washing machine, swimming-pool steps and part of a car wash all united in history by their use of water. From the gallery you enter the main body of the museum where the pumping engines are housed in a completely different atmosphere of stately splendour and they illustrate a specific slice of history. The heroes of the piece are undoubtedly the majestic Cornish Beam Engines, two of which can be seen in action every weekend around 3–3.30 p.m. One of them is the oldest in the world and the other one, the Grand Junction 90, is the world's largest working beam engine which, during its working life from the early 1800s to 1944, would pump six and a half million gallons of water per day to West London's reservoirs via the giant water tower outside. Iron steps allow you to view the machine from its great height and it is impossible not to be impressed by this colossal feat of engineering with the giant beams themselves having been cast in sand moulds with each one being one continuous piece of metal – something that would no longer be attempted in this day and age.

We were lucky enough to be joined at this stage by the museum's education officer who revealed many fascinating snippets of information about the engines in a way that brought them to life for the children and then proceeded to act as an unscheduled personal guide to the rest of the museum. Did you know that the term 'trunk roads' comes from the roads alongside which the elm wood tree trunk water pipes of years ago were laid? While you're there take a look outside at the water-wheel in operation and the water tower itself. All the museum's volunteer staff are unfailingly friendly and are real enthusiasts and this museum makes for an out-of-the-ordinary well-priced outing.

There is a programme of special events including the operation of the Bagnall steam locomotive around the building's perimeter and the chance to climb the giant Stand Pipe Tower so phone for details.

HOW TO GET THERE AND WHERE TO PARK

Car: Follow the North Circular Road (A406) to Chiswick roundabout and then Kew Bridge Road (A205) towards Kew. Take the second road on the right which is Green Dragon Lane and the entrance is immediately on the left-hand side (look for the big tower). There is limited free parking on the site.

Underground: The nearest station is Gunnersbury (District line) from where you take a 237 or 267 bus. Alternatively you can take a 391 bus from Kew Gardens station (District line).

Train: Kew Bridge station is conveniently situated about a ten-minute walk from the museum. Trains leave from London Waterloo via Clapham Junction.

OPENING HOURS

All year, daily, 11 a.m.–5 p.m.
Closed: 25–26 December; Good Friday.
Engines in steam at weekends and bank holiday Mondays.

ADMISSION

Weekends (engines in steam): Adults: £3.25. Children, senior citizens and students: £2.80. Family ticket (two adults and two children): £8.50.
Weekdays (engines static): Adults, children, senior citizens and students: £2. Family ticket (two adults and two children): £5. Children under-12 must be accompanied by an adult.

WHEELCHAIR AND PUSHCHAIR ACCESS

There is access to most of the main parts of the museum, including a lift from the lower-ground floor housing the Water For Life gallery to the ground floor. No access to the upper viewing levels of the beam engines.

REFRESHMENTS

There is a small café which is only open at weekends and bank holidays from 11 a.m. to 5 p.m. It offers a fairly limited but well-priced selection including some good old-fashioned iced buns, scones, carrot cake and doughnuts from around 80p, bacon sandwiches at £1.80 and sandwiches from £1.60. Tea is 50p, coffee is 70p, cans are 70p and fruit juice is 60p. There are no high-chairs and bringing your own food would be frowned on

77

in the café, but there is a picnic area on a gallery in the steam hall or outside by the water-wheel.

SHOP
Located by the entrance and stocking a range of books themed around engines, railways, mines and Cornwall plus a few historical books aimed specifically at children. There is some Thomas the Tank Engine merchandise, a few period items and gifts such as mugs and T-shirts but not a great selection of pocket-money toys.

TOILET FACILITIES
Fairly basic with no baby-changing facilities.

CLOAKROOM
There is no cloakroom but the helpful staff will allow you to leave unwanted bags or buggies behind the counter at the entrance.

PHOTOGRAPHY
Allowed throughout the museum.

DOGS
Guide dogs only.

KNEBWORTH
COUNTRY HOUSE
AND PARK

KNEBWORTH HOUSE, KNEBWORTH, HERTFORDSHIRE, SG3 6PY
TEL: 01438 812661   FAX: 01438 811908

HOW LONG SHOULD WE SPEND THERE?
Allow two to three hours.

WHICH AGE GROUP WILL IT APPEAL TO?
Suitable for all ages.

INTRODUCTION
We have never fully explored the house since our young children are not
very appreciative of stately homes, but we can fully recommend the park
and gardens. Fort Knebworth is a day out in itself; even if you don't explore
the park and house. It is an imaginatively constructed play area within a
wooden enclosure complete with look-out posts, slides and lots of scope
for crawling and climbing, with a soft bark surface underneath for
mishaps. The area is not supervised so young children need to be watched
carefully. Located just outside the fort is the four-run slide where adults
and children alike (including under-fives who can sit with you) can whizz
down on rush mats for free. This is a firm favourite but then there are the
more recently constructed 'Freefall' and 'Corkscrew' slides where parents
tend to opt for observation rather than participation while their braver
children (over-fives only admitted) hurtle down at great speed for the
modest price of £1 for four goes. A free bouncy castle seems to be a
permanent feature in good weather and there are excellent additional
climbing possibilities around the mini assault course. There is even a

79

skateboard and roller-blading half-pipe – although we have never seen it in use.

The miniature railway – which runs in a loop around the grounds, starting from a point near the Fort – charges 90p for adults and 70p for children; and the train will leave when it is full or there are no more takers for the 15-minute round trip. In ten minutes you can be at the house and formal gardens, the gift shop and the café. There is also a chance to buy traditional railway souvenirs such as Thomas the Tank Engine flags. A lively special events calendar means a weekend trip can often coincide with anything from a garden show to a classic car rally throughout the summer. Otherwise, take advantage of the acres of space for ball games and look out for the herds of deer that roam through the park.

HOW TO GET THERE AND WHERE TO PARK

Car: Off junction 7 of the A1(M) near Stevenage then turn left at the roundabout straight into the park entrance. Parking plentiful within the grounds and you can drive the car right up to the Fort boundary.

Train: A 15-minute walk from Knebworth station to the back gate of the park (which is only open at weekends during park admission hours). A taxi would be necessary from Stevenage station, but this would be a weekday option only.

OPENING HOURS

Gardens, Park and Fort Knebworth: 24 March to 15 April, daily, 11 a.m.–5.30 p.m.

24 May to 2 September, daily, 11 a.m.–5.30 p.m.

12 April to 18 May, weekends and bank holidays only, 11 a.m.–5.30 p.m. 6 to 8 September, weekends only, 11 a.m. to 5.30 p.m.

House: Open as above except Mondays, 12 noon–5 p.m. Open bank holiday Mondays, 12 noon–5 p.m.

ADMISSION

House, Gardens, Park and Fort Knebworth inclusive: Adults: £5. Children and senior citizens: £4.50. No family ticket.

Gardens, Park and Fort Knebworth inclusive: Adults and children: £4. Family ticket (four people): £14. Under-fives: free.

WHEELCHAIR AND PUSHCHAIR ACCESS

Slightly difficult over the grassy open slopes in the park but not insurmountable and there is plenty of room in the café. The Fort and play areas are not set up to accommodate wheelchair users, although they are accessible to a wheelchair. The house is not really suitable for wheels and the upper floor is entirely inaccessible to wheelchairs.

REFRESHMENTS
There is a kiosk serving ice-cream and tea and coffee in the Fort. The self-service café at the entrance of the house serves hot and cold food from a rather basic menu (pre-packed sandwiches £1.70, tea 30p) in a charmless 'barn' setting which has a licensed bar, or outside on benches overlooking the fountain. There were no high-chairs. Bringing your own food would not be welcomed at the café, but there are picnic benches at Fort Knebworth and masses of scope for open-air eating in the grassy park.

SHOP
Located by the restaurant this is a very disappointing establishment for such a large-scale operation. There are the usual cheap pads and pens, personalised as Knebworth's own, some home-made jams and chutneys and a more interesting selection of books – but nothing particularly inspiring for children. There is another shop by the house.

TOILET FACILITIES
Portakabins with wheelchair access at Fort Knebworth but no baby-changing facilities. More wheelchair-access toilets at the house entrance, near the shop and café, but surprisingly basic; again with no baby-changing facilities. No wheelchair-access toilets at the house.

CLOAKROOM
No supervised cloakroom for the park, Fort or gardens, but pushchairs and other items could be left at the house entrance if tickets have been bought for the house.

PHOTOGRAPHY
Allowed.

DOGS
Only allowed in the park if kept on a lead.

LEEDS CASTLE

MAIDSTONE, KENT, ME17 1PL
TEL: 01622 765400/01622 880008

HOW LONG SHOULD WE SPEND THERE?
Allow at least three to four hours.

WHICH AGE GROUP WILL IT APPEAL TO?
Suitable for all ages.

INTRODUCTION
Don't be put off by the apparent distance of Leeds Castle from London – we can get there from north London in just under an hour and a half and it is definitely well worth the effort.

The promotional literature proclaims it to be 'the loveliest castle in the world' and while this may seem to be a touch exaggerated, its beautiful setting, built on two small islands in the middle of a lake and surrounded by 500 acres of landscaped parkland, does lend itself to comparison with the Loire chateaux. Its royal history spans several centuries from its 9th-century origins through to when it was rebuilt in the 12th century and on to its place in history when Henry VIII converted it into a royal palace at considerable expense. The castle has, in fact, been owned and run as a charitable trust now for over 20 years and, indeed, is nowadays used also as a residential conference centre. This probably accounts for one of the few disappointing aspects of the visit, namely that not as much of the actual castle is accessible to the public as might be hoped given its size. Those rooms that are open to view, however, are splendid and do give a feeling of warmth and homeliness that is not usually present in such buildings.

There's an excellent exhibition on heraldry, a reconstruction of a queen's bedroom and bathroom as they might have been at the time of

Henry V, a splendid drawing-room, banqueting-room and the more contemporary bedroom of Lady Baillie who was the last private owner of the castle and the longest resident in its history.

The ticket for the grounds alone offers lots to see and do and gives access to the extensive grounds, duckery, aviary, dog collar museum, Culpeper garden, maze, grotto, vineyard and greenhouses. A shelter is currently being built to provide a refuge in bad weather and this will also contain some environmental exhibits. There is also extensive landscaping work taking place to create a new formal garden alongside the lake. Many unusual breeds of duck and geese as well as black swans and pheasants roam freely in the park and the aviary is surprisingly large, populated mainly with birds from warmer climes with exotically coloured plumage such as macaws, toucans and parrots. The Culpeper garden is at its best in the spring but the yew-tree maze laid out in the shape of a queen's crown and the beautiful grotto full of shell and stone sculptures at its centre can be enjoyed at any time. A vineyard was recorded on the site of the present vineyard in the Domesday Book and its products are available in the restaurant and shops.

The castle has a year-round programme of special events such as open-air concerts, fireworks displays, children's half-term activities, New Year treasure trail (recommended), Easter egg hunt and the truly spectacular hot-air balloon and vintage car fiesta – a leaflet is available detailing all of these.

The castle is quite a walk from the car-park so if you are not feeling energetic take the courtesy bus.

HOW TO GET THERE AND WHERE TO PARK

Car: Located four miles east of Maidstone. The castle is well signposted off the M20 at junction 8 then follow the A20 which is signed all the way. There is a huge amount of free parking space in the grounds with a special car-park close to the ticket office for orange badge holders.

Train: Connex South Eastern and Leeds Castle run a daily combined entrance scheme from stations in London (Victoria) and the south-east. There is a regular shuttle bus service from Bearsted and Hollingbourne stations.

OPENING HOURS

November to February, daily, 10 a.m.–3 p.m.* (Castle opens at 10.15 a.m.)
March to October, daily, 10 a.m.–5 p.m.* (Castle opens 11 a.m.)
*Last admission to the grounds which close two hours later.
Closed: 25 December.

83

ADMISSION

Castle, park and gardens: Adults: £8.50, £6.50. Children (5–15): £5.50. Senior citizens and students:£6.50. Family ticket (up to two adults and three children): £23.

Park and gardens: Adults: £6.50. Children (5–15): £4. Senior citizens and students: £5. Family ticket (up to two adults and three children): £19.

There is also something called a Castle Card which gives 12 months unlimited access to the castle, park and gardens and, as with the normal admission charges, also includes entrance to all day-time special events. Call the Castle for full details.

WHEELCHAIR AND PUSHCHAIR ACCESS

The grounds are superbly laid out to allow easy access. There is a special information leaflet available at the ticket office giving full details of facilities for the disabled – among which is a mini-bus service from the ticket office to the castle entrance. The castle itself is best accessed by the front door as the usual entrance involves two sets of steps. Pushchairs do, however, have to be left inside the front door before proceeding further. Pushchairs are not allowed in the maze and the grotto which simply cannot accommodate any kind of wheels at all. The Fairfax Hall restaurant can be accessed easily but the tables and chairs are rather cramped making manoeuvring a little tricky; there is some space to store wheelchairs and pushchairs if preferred.

REFRESHMENTS

The Fairfax Hall bar and self-service restaurant is a pleasant brick and wood barn building serving wholesome food. Hot food includes chilli at £4.95, lamb and apricot casserole at £5.50 and home-made soup at £1.45. Baked potatoes start at £1.45 and come with a range of fillings, sandwiches are perhaps a little pricey starting at £2.15 and there's a wide choice of cakes such as cheesecake, treacle tart or carrot cake starting at £1.30. Coffee, a pot of tea, fresh fruit juice and soft drinks are all 90p. There are a few high-chairs available but it is a busy restaurant and it could be difficult to secure one. The restaurant is licensed with wine by the glass costing £1.80.

There are tables outside in the courtyard for fine weather but the main picnic area is a grassy area with tables and benches adjacent to the ticket office and close to the main car-park; picnics are not allowed in the castle grounds. There is also a refreshment stall serving ice-cream and drinks close to the car-park and ticket office.

SHOP

There are four shops, the main ones being the two located in the Fairfax Hall courtyard and the one by the ticket office. One of the shops is dedicated almost exclusively to clothes while the others stock a superior range of gifts including some lovely children's books and games, pottery, toiletries, confectionery, preserves, stationery and some beautiful greetings cards. The shops all stock the official Leeds Castle guidebook which is available in a wide range of languages including Mandarin!

TOILET FACILITIES

There are toilets with wheelchair access and family rooms with baby-changing facilities by the ticket office and adjacent to the Fairfax Hall courtyard. The toilets in the Fairfax Hall restaurant do not have specific baby-changing facilities but there is a wide bench/table if you have a portable changing mat.

CLOAKROOM

There are a few unlockable left-luggage lockers at the lychgate by the ticket office. These are under the constant watch of the entrance staff but are not big enough for pushchairs.

PHOTOGRAPHY

No photography or video recording is allowed inside the castle, but it is permitted around the grounds.

DOGS

Guide dogs only (even in the grounds).

LEGOLAND
WINDSOR

WINDSOR, BERKSHIRE, SL4 4AY
TEL: 01753 626111

HOW LONG SHOULD WE SPEND THERE?
Allow all day.

WHICH AGE GROUP WILL IT APPEAL TO?
Suitable for all ages.

INTRODUCTION
Although expensive, this sophisticated and professional theme park earns a place alongside the well-established competition. An early start is recommended to beat the queues but this is made more bearable by whiling away the time until opening (having already purchased tickets) in the Hilltop café. The indoor interactive area was popular, especially the simulated earthquake pad and the track where children vied with adults to make and race their own model vehicles. The main model area, themed around typical snapshot scenes from various countries and cities, is truly impressive in its detail – although the amazing statistics dotted at intervals around the area, such as the man hours required to build certain models – will be lost on those small children who cannot conceive of anything longer than a day. Still, their appreciation of the miniature is undiminished. Other attractions include a 'helicopter' ride, mazes, fairground rides, a motorbike room, a fairy-tale boat ride, spinning spiders and a minor white-knuckle ride which will be unimpressive to those weaned on scarier stuff. Highlights included panning for gold where, for the extra cost of a pound, the children can earn themselves a medal to take home and the car-racing tracks for both

older children and 'learners'. Look out for the show times, especially Imagination Theatre and My Town Harbour. A unique, child-driven place and a great day out.

HOW TO GET THERE AND WHERE TO PARK
Car: Junction 6 off M4 then signposted to Legoland. Car-parking plentiful and free within the grounds, but it does get very crowded in summer.
Train: To Windsor Riverside or Central then there is a shuttle-bus service which runs every 30 minutes for £11 return.

OPENING HOURS
21 March to 2 November, daily. Car-park gates open at 9 a.m. Ticket office opens at 9.30 a.m. Park opens 10 a.m.–6 p.m., except in July and August when it closes at 8 p.m.

ADMISSION
Adults: £15. Children (3–15): £12. Under-threes: free. Senior citizens: £11. No family ticket.

WHEELCHAIR AND PUSHCHAIR ACCESS
Excellent access throughout the park, and pushchairs can be hired for a small charge. Wheelchair hire is free. Almost all rides have a separate wheelchair gate and attendants will help to transfer customers to the rides.

REFRESHMENTS
There are plenty of places to eat, including snack stalls, and the general quality of food seemed to be high. For example, the Hilltop café, decorated in glorious primaries, served Danish pastries and fresh fruit salad; bacon rolls sizzled as you watched but with fresh orange juice at £1.80 and cappuccino at £1.20, it isn't cheap. Everything from the crockery to the cheerful attitude of the staff has been thought about, but oddly there is nowhere to rest your tray as you walk around the self-service counters. So, be warned, unless you are extremely dexterous and can balance food, steer the buggy and keep hold of wayward toddlers all at the same time. Highchairs are available. Bringing your own food is not discouraged outside the restaurants and there are plenty of outdoor picnic benches scattered around the park and in the Picnic Grove.

SHOP
There are several shops throughout the park, all relentlessly merchandising Legoland souvenirs. However, there is, as one would expect, much

Lego amongst the sweatshirts, mugs, pencils, etc. and this makes a better take-home gift than many of the usual offers.

TOILET FACILITIES
These are exceptional. The décor follows the same primaries theme and not only do they have separate disabled facilities and baby-changing facilities in the ladies' and men's, in a separate family room there are also child-height pegs, taps, mirrors and dryers. There is also a special mother-and-baby centre for quiet feeding.

CLOAKROOM
None, but there are coin-operated lockers at the entrance.

PHOTOGRAPHY
Allowed and film is sold at the entrance and at all the shops throughout the park.

DOGS
Dogs are not allowed within the park (except guide dogs), but there are kennels which are available free of charge.

LITTLE VENICE CANAL RIDES

OPPOSITE NO 60 BLOMFIELD ROAD,
LITTLE VENICE, LONDON, W9 2PD
TEL: 0171 286 3428

HOW LONG SHOULD WE SPEND THERE?
Allow all day.

WHICH AGE GROUP WILL IT APPEAL TO?
Suitable for all ages.

INTRODUCTION
A wonderful summer's day outing is to take the traditionally painted *Jason* or *Holland* narrow boats from Little Venice to Camden Lock along the Regent's Park Canal. The trip takes 45 minutes one way and a guide points out all the interesting sites along the route. Children too young to appreciate this will still enjoy simply being aboard. Have lunch at Camden Lock, where many of the numerous cafés, restaurants and snack bars are happy to accommodate children, and while away the afternoon browsing through the vibrant weekend market before you take the boat back (check at Little Venice for return times before leaving). Be warned: the market is very busy at weekends and it is not easy to get a buggy around, but older children will delight in the frantic activity. We do recommend doing the journey this way round as there is little to occupy you at Little Venice – other than the restaurant – while you wait for the return trip. Try to go on a fine day as, although the boats are covered, wandering around Camden in the rain is not much fun.

HOW TO GET THERE AND WHERE TO PARK

Car: There is no off-street parking in the vicinity so parking is limited to a few meters nearby. There appears to be less of a problem on Sundays when the meters are free, but be warned on weekdays, you will have to search for a space and pay high meter charges.

Underground: Five-minute walk from Warwick Avenue station.

Bus: Bus routes 6 and 46.

OPENING HOURS

Open all week for information and group bookings but scheduled departures run as follows:

April to May, daily, 10.30 a.m., 12.30 p.m., 2.30 p.m.

June, July, August, daily, 10.30 a.m., 12.30 p.m., 2.30 p.m. Also at 4.30 p.m. on weekends and bank holidays only.

September, daily, 10.30 a.m., 12.30 p.m., 2.30 p.m.

October, daily, 12.30 p.m., 2.30 p.m.

ADMISSION

Adults, return: £5.50, single: £4.50. Children (14 and under), return: £4, single: £3. Family return (two adults and two children): £16. Under-threes: free. Senior citizens pay the child fare on Monday to Saturday.

WHEELCHAIR AND PUSHCHAIR ACCESS

Wheelchairs can't be accommodated on the boat but, with advance warning, the crew are very happy to lift passengers on board in one of their regular chairs. Wheelchairs and pushchairs are stored on the roof during the journey and you are asked to seat small children on your lap if there are no other free places.

REFRESHMENTS

The canalside restaurant sells drinks and biscuits over the counter, and if you fancy something more substantial they have a brasserie-type menu during the day. Prices range from £1 for coffee and £2.25 for a cake to simple but tasty dishes for £5. Children are welcome if they are well behaved. However, the evening menu is a much more adult affair at £35 a head. There are no high-chairs. The restaurant opens in summer at around 9 a.m., but in autumn may not open until 2 p.m. and would close at around 4 p.m. opening again at 6.30 p.m. for dinner. On board, cream teas and salad lunches can be booked in advance at a cost of between £4 and £9 per person or you can simply purchase canned drinks, biscuits and crisps. You will not be thrown off the boat if you eat your own food!

SHOP
No.

TOILET FACILITIES
There are toilets with wheelchair access at the destination point in Little Venice. There are no special baby-changing facilities, although there was a flat cupboard surface that would suffice. Toilets on board but with no wheelchair access.

CLOAKROOM
No.

PHOTOGRAPHY
No restrictions. No film sold.

DOGS
Tolerated if small and well behaved.

LONDON AQUARIUM

COUNTY HALL, RIVERSIDE BUILDING,
WESTMINSTER BRIDGE ROAD, LONDON, SE1 7PB
TEL: 0171 967 8000   FAX: 0171 967 8029

HOW LONG SHOULD WE SPEND THERE?
Allow two hours.

WHICH AGE GROUP WILL IT APPEAL TO?
Suitable for all ages.

INTRODUCTION
We experienced long queues to get in on a blisteringly hot summer's day, so it probably pays to get there early. The Aquarium is divided into three levels, all dimly lit to simulate an underwater environment with each zone accompanied by appropriate background noise as you wind your way through European Freshwater to the Indian Ocean, Reef and Living Corals and Tropical Freshwater and Rainforest displays amongst others. The Atlantic is depicted by a huge three-storey-high tank where you can see stingrays, conger eels and smooth hound sharks which thrill by swimming tantalisingly close to the glass. The Discovery Zone is a good idea but I suspect it may once have been better stocked with starfish, mussels and crabs which you are supposed to be able to touch. The marine life was a little sparse, making the experience a little frustrating and, judging by the crowd of kids clamouring to get near, most of the molluscs have probably expired from shock by now. The harmless rays in the pier tank fare a little better and it is quite thrilling to put your hands in the cold water and feel them brush against your fingers. They are almost exhibitionist in their habit of swimming just out of reach and

performing aquabatics. Small children will have to be lifted up to this one but many of the tanks come down to floor level and some have 'step' levels. The illuminated signs are good on the whole – although many of the tanks appeared not to hold the creatures listed, or had unidentified inhabitants. A lot of effort has been made to make the tanks appear interesting and many contain mock ruined sculptures which are appropriate to the area of the globe you would be in. Occasional video screens give additional information and there is a series of presentations throughout the day.

HOW TO GET THERE AND WHERE TO PARK
Car: Parking is limited to on-street parking or at Waterloo station.

Underground: Ten-minute walk from Waterloo station – but it is very badly signposted. Take the exit closest to the Eurostar ticket desks, head for Westminster Bridge and then take the steps on the right down to the riverside walk, just before you would cross the bridge heading for the houses of Parliament. Also close to Westminster tube.

Train: As above from Waterloo station.

OPENING HOURS
All year, Monday to Friday, 10 a.m.–6 p.m. Weekends, 9.30 a.m.–6 p.m. Bank Holidays, 9.30 a.m.–7.30 p.m.

Closed: 25 December.

ADMISSION
Adults: £6.50. Children (3–14): £4.50. Students, senior citizens and the unemployed: £5.50. Family ticket (two adults and two children): £20. Wheelchair users: free.

WHEELCHAIR AND PUSHCHAIR ACCESS
It is very difficult to negotiate the steps from Westminster Bridge with a pushchair and impossible with a wheelchair, so the best route is through Jubilee Gardens. All areas of the gallery are fully accessible to wheelchair users and it is easy to manoeuvre through the wide aisles. There are lifts to all of the three floors.

REFRESHMENTS
The Globe café, located beyond the shop, is open from 11 a.m.–6 p.m. but its only recommendation is the view over the Thames to Big Ben. It has unimaginative fare; expensive sandwiches at £2.50, hot-dogs at £1.95 and pizza slices at £2.35. Coffee is 95p, tea 85p and fresh orange juice £1.50.

The service was very poor. Opt for the free view and take your own food to eat on the benches outside.

SHOP
The shop is open daily from 10 a.m. on weekdays and 9.30 a.m. at the weekend. It has a good selection of gifts, toys, games and books, all of which have a marine link.

TOILET FACILITIES
Wheelchair access on each of the three levels but baby-changing facilities are on the basement level only.

CLOAKROOM
No.

PHOTOGRAPHY
Not allowed.

DOGS
Guide dogs only.

LONDON CANAL MUSEUM

12-13 NEW WHARF ROAD, LONDON, N1 9RT
TEL: 0171 713 0836

HOW LONG SHOULD WE SPEND THERE?
Allow about an hour.

WHICH AGE GROUP WILL IT APPEAL TO?
Suitable for all ages.

INTRODUCTION
A small and very specialised museum which captures a unique slice of London's history while explaining about the once essential British inland waterway system.

How many of us are aware of the existence of the Regents Canal but know precious little about it? Perhaps this is because it was deliberately constructed in a gully and partly hidden so that the dirty and often bare-chested workers did not offend the refined gaze of London's upper classes. Considerable wall space is devoted to the history of the museum building which was originally constructed in 1857 as an ice-house for the nineteenth-century ice magnate Carlo Gatti. Indeed the building was connected with the ice trade until the mid-1920s. To appreciate this gem of information from Victorian history you have to remember that ice was not an accessible commodity until the later construction of mechanical ice-making machines. It was, nonetheless, in high demand by butchers and householders as the only way to keep food fresh, so much so that a considerable trade sprang up around the importing of ice from Norway. The ice was brought up the canal to be stored in Gatti's two 40-foot-deep ice wells beneath the museum. Only one of these wells has been partially excavated and remains the only visible one of its kind in Britain.

The long-term plan is to fully excavate both wells when funds and volunteers are available, in order to create a permanent exhibition on the ice and ice-cream trades; in the meantime we found a temporary exhibition on display devoted to the history of ice-cream making in Britain.

Most of the museum is, of course, dedicated to the canal and its essential workhorse, the narrow boat. There isn't much interactivity – acknowledged by the charitable trust who run it and reflected in the very reasonable price for children – but you can explore the tiny living-quarters of a traditional narrow boat, play with a model lock (water not included) and our children were surprisingly entertained by pressing the buttons on the huge canal map to see different sections of waterway light up.

In the upstairs exhibition area – converted from the original hayloft and stables which were used when ice was delivered by horse-drawn cart – there's a potted history of the Thames from the Ice Age, appropriately enough, to the present day, as well as displays on the problems of educating canal children, the role of women on the canals and anecdotes about canal life. An informative video points out a wealth of interesting facts about the canal and highlights many places of interest along its route from Little Venice to the Limehouse Basin. The museum also has a continuous programme of exhibitions and lectures.

If you're visiting the Canal Museum you may also like to visit one of the area's curiosities, the Camley Street Natural Park (12 Camley Street, London, NW1, tel: 0171 833 2311), and if the back of the King's Cross station is the last place you would expect to find a wildlife sanctuary then you'll be pleasantly surprised. There is in fact a connection with the museum as the Regent's Canal flows past the park too, and it is water from the canal that fills the park's ponds, reed beds and marsh area; these are actively managed to attract wildlife and are a haven for many types of birds and insects, as well as water dwellers such as toads and newts.

The park is small but there is a circular path around it which takes the visitor through the flower meadow, woodland area and garden beds. There is also a visitor centre full of information about the park, its inhabitants and the work of the London Wildlife Trust.

Entrance to the park is free but dogs and cycling are not permitted. The park is also a community resource and has a regular programme of events such as family fun days and the park's own birthday festival.

HOW TO GET THERE AND WHERE TO PARK

Car: Off Wharfdale Road. There is only on-street parking in the area which is very restricted except on Sundays.

Underground: A five-minute walk from King's Cross and St Pancras stations (Piccadilly, Northern, Victoria, Metropolitan and Circle lines).

Train: A five-minute walk from King's Cross and St Pancras stations.

OPENING HOURS

Museum: All year, Tuesday to Sunday, 10 a.m.–4.30 p.m. (last admission 3.45 p.m.).

Closed: 1 January, 24–26 December.

Park: Summer, Monday to Thursday, 9 a.m.–5 p.m. Weekends, 11 a.m.–5 p.m. Winter, Monday to Thursday, 9 a.m.–5 p.m. Weekends, 10 a.m.–4 p.m.

Closed: Fridays.

ADMISSION

Museum: Adults: £2.50. Children, senior citizens, unemployed and students: £1.25. Under-eights free.

Park: Free.

WHEELCHAIR AND PUSHCHAIR ACCESS

There are stairs to the upper floor making access for wheels almost impossible unless pushchairs are carried. There is no lift.

REFRESHMENTS

There is no café but tea and coffee, priced 40p, are thoughtfully provided for a do-it-yourself service.

SHOP

A small shop by the entrance sells a selection of waterways-related books, traditional painted metalware, pottery and Rosie and Jim merchandise.

TOILET FACILITIES

No disabled toilet or baby-changing facilities.

CLOAKROOM

No.

PHOTOGRAPHY
Allowed throughout the museum.

DOGS
Guide dogs only.

LONDON DUNGEON

TOOLEY STREET, LONDON, SE1
TEL: 0171 403 0606 (RECORDED INFORMATION)/0171 403 7221
FAX: 0171 378 1529

HOW LONG SHOULD WE SPEND THERE?
Allow two hours.

WHICH AGE GROUP WILL IT APPEAL TO?
Not suitable for under-fives or the squeamish of any age.

INTRODUCTION
We went with much trepidation after our only partially successful visit to
the Chamber of Horrors at Madame Tussaud's, but I can honestly say that
the children seemed to thrive on the frisson of fearful expectation – even
though I would have deemed the whole thing unsuitable.

Prepare yourself for a possible half-hour wait to get in, and beware of
the hideously made-up attendants and the semi-darkness. There are lots of
warning notices at the entrance and it would pay to take heed. It is truly
macabre, whether you're gawping with horror at the ingenuity of
graphically illustrated medieval torture or experiencing the terrors of
Newgate Prison in the 17th century. Little cameos show the execution of
Mary, Queen of Scots, and Anne Boleyn, using holograms and the murder
of Thomas à Becket is gruesomely depicted. The predominant colours are
black and red, the smells putrid, and the noises like old Hammer horror
movies. You're ushered into a kangaroo court where a judge condemns you
to death for what could have been any one of a long list of offences
punishable by death two centuries ago – including stealing a pocket
handkerchief. You then board a boat for a journey to execution down the
River of Death which is quite terrifying. The Jack the Ripper section is
predictably horrific with no holds barred, but the *pièce de résistance* has

to be the execution by guillotine and its vivid aftermath experienced in pitch darkness – I'll leave the rest to your imagination.

A colour guidebook costs £1.50, but you'll be hard pushed to read it in the gloom.

HOW TO GET THERE AND WHERE TO PARK
Car: Car-park at the London Bridge end of Tooley Street. On-street parking in Tooley Street at weekends.
Underground: Two-minute walk from London Bridge station.
Train: As above.

OPENING HOURS
All year, daily, 10 a.m.–5.30 p.m. (Last admission 4.30 p.m.)
Closed: 25 December.

ADMISSION
Adults: £8.95. Children: £6.50. Students: £7.95. Senior citizens: £6.50. Child prices for wheelchair users and carers.

WHEELCHAIR AND PUSHCHAIR ACCESS
Full access to all areas, but wheelchair users are only allowed on the boat ride if they can get on with the help of a carer.

REFRESHMENTS
Not what you would call a classy joint with a Pizza Hut serving the usual reasonably priced fare; pizza slice with half baked potato and salad £2.80, coffee 79p, tea 69p, soft drinks from 79p, pizza slice from £1.25, baked potatoes, crisps and cakes; with the added twist of being able to eat your meal at a table decorated with severed heads.

SHOP
As would be expected some good Hallowe'en material, goosebump books, London Dungeon souvenirs, jewellery, sweets, and pocket-money toys.

TOILET FACILITIES
Wheelchair-access toilets and baby-changing facilities available (although the concept of taking a baby to a place like this is an interesting one!).

CLOAKROOM
No.

PHOTOGRAPHY
Not possible.

DOGS
Not allowed.

THE LONDON TOY AND MODEL MUSEUM

21-23 CRAVEN HILL, LONDON, W2 3EN
TEL: 0171 402 5222 (RECORDED INFORMATION)/0171 706 8000

HOW LONG SHOULD WE SPEND THERE?
Allow two hours.

WHICH AGE GROUP WILL IT APPEAL TO?
Suitable for all ages.

INTRODUCTION
A delightful day out and one of the most carefully created museums we have visited. Two large Victorian houses have been converted into 20 themed galleries displaying over 7,000 items. It's well worth picking up the first-class and exquisitely produced catalogue at £2.50 which will guide you through the various rooms from the ships and boats gallery (themed as a ship's deck) to the games room (dominated by a huge wall-mounted snakes and ladders board) all the way to the Penny Arcade. The museum is filled with exhibits from years ago to the present day and the rooms echo with parents' and grandparents' cries of 'I had one of those!'. Each room has been created with immense attention to detail from the walls to the floors. The exhibits themselves are well labelled and the catalogue provides extra information on the general history and development of the items in each gallery. There are lots of interactive displays throughout the museum and loose change is needed to operate one or two exhibits. Highlights include the working model funfair and coal mine each of which dominate a room of their own but, without a doubt, the star turn for our kids was the

Alpine model railway which runs to a timetable throughout the day. Finish the visit with free rides on the miniature railway and 1920s roundabout. There is nothing remotely shabby about this beautiful building and its fascinating museum.

HOW TO GET THERE AND WHERE TO PARK

Car: Limited on-street meter parking (single yellow lines on Sundays) and car-park at Lancaster Gate (a ten-minute walk to the museum).

Underground: an easy walk from Paddington, Bayswater, Lancaster Gate or Queensway stations.

Train: Paddington station.

Bus: Routes 12 and 94 to Lancaster Gate, 7, 15, 23 and 36 to Paddington.

OPENING HOURS

All year, Monday to Saturday, 10 a.m.–5.30 p.m. Sunday and bank holidays, 11 a.m.–5.30 p.m. (Last admission 4.40 p.m.)
Closed: 1 January, 25–26 December.

ADMISSION

Adults: £4.95. Children (4–16): £2.95. Concessions: £3.95. Under-fours: free. Family ticket (two adults and two children): £13.50.

WHEELCHAIR AND PUSHCHAIR ACCESS

The museum never gained planning permission to put lifts throughout the building so wheelchair and buggy access is extremely limited and not recommended. There is a lift to the basement only (just one of four floors). This makes managing with a baby and a toddler – who may need lifting to see certain exhibits – very difficult if you're on your own.

REFRESHMENTS

The conservatory café opens with the museum and closes at 4.30 p.m. It serves a variety of hot and cold food (stops serving hot food at 2.30 p.m.). Prices are reasonable at £1.20 to £1.80 for sandwiches, with cartons and cans of drink costing 60p. The hot-food menu is fairly extensive and includes soup (£1.50), baked potatoes (£2.50), burgers and pizzas from £2.25 and cream tea is also served at £4.50. You're welcome to eat your own food inside the café and the garden has several benches for picnics. We spotted two high-chairs. The room can be hired for parties so don't expect peace and quiet!

SHOP

Well stocked and displayed with a range of gifts from pocket-money toys to teddies, traditional wooden toys, model cars, Dorling and Kindersley books and sweatshirts. Not cheap but some good-quality ideas.

TOILET FACILITIES

There are toilets at the entrance and a separate room with baby-changing facilities for use by adults of either sex. None have wheelchair or buggy access. There are more toilets with baby-changing facilities and wheelchair access in the basement by the shop and café.

CLOAKROOM

Free and unsupervised cloakroom area with space for buggies.

PHOTOGRAPHY

Allowed but no film sold.

DOGS

Guide dogs only.

LONDON TRANSPORT MUSEUM

COVENT GARDEN, LONDON, WC2E 7BB
TEL: 0171 836 8557 (24-HOUR RECORDED INFORMATION)/
0171 379 6344 (ADMINISTRATION)

HOW LONG SHOULD WE SPEND THERE?
Allow two to three hours.

WHICH AGE GROUP WILL IT APPEAL TO?
Suitable for all ages.

INTRODUCTION
Housed in a iron-framed hall which was once London's central flower market, this is a superbly laid out exhibition which covers the development of London's transport system from its inception to the present day. You can opt for a guided tour or do-it-yourself, exploring horse-drawn carriages, buses and tube trains, many of which are there to be clambered on. Most major displays have touch-screen information databases in several languages. Alternatively, a few attendants in period costume will talk about the exhibits. The simulator where budding tube train drivers (of all ages) can try out their skills was a big success! The museum is owned by London Transport so do not expect any car lovers here; the video voice-overs and text accompaniments are strongly biased in favour of a government-funded transport policy and put forward well-reasoned arguments in favour of this – not least the environmental angle. There is a schoolroom where the children can draw and do quizzes and the museum operates a comprehensive programme of activities throughout the year

(you can pick up a programme at reception or phone in advance). On the day we arrived the lecture room was hosting a hands-on animal encounter where a visiting London Zoo keeper allowed various furry and spiky creatures to have human encounters. An interactive and well-thought-out exhibition and one the children would be happy to visit again and again.

HOW TO GET THERE AND WHERE TO PARK

Car: The museum has no designated car-park and parking is very restricted with limited local meter space. The nearest multi-storey car-park is conveniently situated on Parker Street, about a ten-minute walk from the museum, but allow for central London parking charges.

Underground: Five-minute walk from Covent Garden station.

Train: Fifteen-minute walk from Charing Cross station.

OPENING HOURS

All year, daily (except Friday), 10 a.m.–6 p.m. Friday, 11 a.m.–6 p.m. (Last entry 5.15 p.m.)

Closed: 24–26 December.

ADMISSION

Adults: £4.50. Children (5–15), students, senior citizens, disabled and unemployed: £2.50. Family ticket (two adults and two children): £11. Under-fives: free.

WHEELCHAIR AND PUSHCHAIR ACCESS

Excellent wheelchair and pushchair access throughout the museum with lifts to the upper floor, wide aisles and ramps.

REFRESHMENTS

Bright café which is open 10 a.m.–6 p.m. situated on two levels with seating for around 50 people overlooking Covent Garden Piazza. Opening hours match the museum's and there are high-chairs. Prices are reasonable for central London with cold drinks at £1, sandwiches for £2 and café fare such as cream teas, soup and pastries. You are not allowed to consume your own food on the premises but on a fine day you could picnic on the benches in the Piazza just outside or there is a multitude of local eateries to suit most tastes and budgets.

SHOP

Excellent gift shop (opening hours as museum) with everything related to transport from pocket-money toys to the more sophisticated (and ubiquitous) London Transport advertising posters from over the years that now seem to adorn everything, including t-shirts and postcards.

TOILET FACILITIES
The museum toilet facilities have both wheelchair access and a good parent-and-baby room. There are additional facilities in the café also with wheelchair access but no baby-changing facilities.

CLOAKROOM
Free-of-charge, supervised cloakroom with lots of room for buggies.

PHOTOGRAPHY
Allowed and film sold at reception desk.

DOGS
Guide dogs only.

LONDON ZOO

REGENT'S PARK, LONDON, NW1
TEL: 0171 722 3333 (24-HOUR INFORMATION)/0891 505 767 (ZOO LINE)

HOW LONG SHOULD WE SPEND THERE?
Allow four hours.

WHICH AGE GROUP WILL IT APPEAL TO?
Suitable for all ages.

INTRODUCTION
London Zoo remains a firm favourite and although we prefer to see the animals in the wider spaces of a wildlife park, it's also worth bearing in mind that many of the animals here have been rescued from far worse enclosures and many are close to extinction. There's a tremendous emphasis on educational conservation now including practical measures like breeding programmes, so there's lots to see and learn with the informative signs to help. There is a huge variety here from the aquarium to the reptile house, the invertebrates, otters, moonlight animals and pet-care centre, as well as the aviary and all the larger, more traditional zoo animals. It's well worth picking up a daily events programme at the ticket kiosk or information booth and planning your visit around the talks and animal encounters: they vary seasonally but you can do things like meet the lion and bear keepers, watch an elephant being weighed and washed down, see the penguins being fed or feed the pigs yourself and much more. There are pony and camel rides, a couple of toddlers' play areas, an excellent centre near the penguins where you can paint your own plaster animal souvenir and a craft centre next to the picnic shop where you can make your own badges. For a programme of summer workshops call 0171 722 3333.

HOW TO GET THERE AND WHERE TO PARK

Car: Car-park in Regent's Park on the Outer Circle just north of the main zoo entrance with a daily rate of £4 with zoo visitor's discount. Otherwise take your chances on the main roads in the park but they do get very busy.

Underground: Closest station is Camden Town but it's at least 30 minutes' walk.

Canal: London water bus along Regent's canal.

OPENING HOURS

School holidays, weekends and bank holidays, daily, 10 a.m.–5.30 p.m. Other times, daily, 10 a.m.–4 p.m.
Closed: 25 December.

ADMISSION

Adults: £8. Children (4–10): £6. Students and senior citizens: £6.50. No family ticket. Under-fours free.

WHEELCHAIR AND PUSHCHAIR ACCESS

Very few areas are not accessible to wheels, with wide spaces hampered only by other pushchairs (it does get busy!). Pushchair and wheelchair hire at the entrance.

REFRESHMENTS

Relatively expensive and not wonderful. Lots of ice-cream and snack kiosks with soft drinks from 95p, small portion of chips at £1.15 and six mini-doughnuts for 90p. The picnic shop sells sandwiches starting at £2.35. The Fountain café serves basic fare and is very child-friendly with baby food and even nappies for sale. There's a grassy area for picnics near Barclay Court with lots of benches or opt for a picnic in the adjacent Regent's Park where the kids can have a real run-around.

SHOP

A large, fun shop stocked with a vast selection of great and difficult-to-resist goodies with an animal theme. Choose from videos, badges, stuffed toys, stamp kits, crayons, books and much, much more.

TOILET FACILITIES

Located throughout the zoo.

CLOAKROOM
Yes.

PHOTOGRAPHY
Allowed. Film sold.

DOGS
Guide dogs only.

THE LOOK OUT
DISCOVERY PARK

NINE MILE RIDE, BRACKNELL, BERKSHIRE, RG12 7QW
TEL: 01344 868222

HOW LONG SHOULD WE SPEND THERE?
Allow two and a half hours to all day.

WHICH AGE GROUP WILL IT APPEAL TO?
Suitable for all ages.

INTRODUCTION
A relatively new and exciting enterprise set in 2,600 acres of Crown Estate woodland. The Discovery Outpost consists of a first-class indoor exploration area for the kids broken down into five different zones called sound and communication, light and colour, body and perception, forces and movement and woodland and nature. Although not enormous, the place is packed with one interactive exhibit after another. In fact exhibit is too static a word to describe these instructional and creative games. You can crawl along a mole hole, shout down the echo tube, photograph your shadow, build a body, make a beach ball hover in mid-air and many more exciting activities. The scientific principle behind each one is then explained. We spent two hours in here, but you can make an even fuller day by taking one of the trail walks in the surrounding woodland. These range from an easy one-mile stroll to a four-mile nature trail, although most of the trails could be described as walks for softies and are not taxing. A map is available at reception for 25p and you can then take your pick.

If you're feeling really energetic you can take your bikes on the special trails (up to eight miles) but you need a permit for the day; alternatively you can hire good-quality bikes there (tel: 01344 772797) from 10 a.m. to dusk all year. However, beware, the mountain bike trail is more demanding than it looks with steep hills and very uneven ground which is taxing for the adults let alone small children. Safety helmets are a must and complete novices may be better advised to avoid this altogether.

If you don't want to stray too far afield there is a superb secure and dog-free play area located right next to the centre with excellent wooden apparatus on a soft bark surface with an infants' area themed as a play trail and a more demanding enclosure for the over-sevens. In any case a great diversion for those who finish their picnic early.

Another option is to combine a visit to the Outpost with a visit to the Coral Reef adventure pool just over the road. In fact at certain times of the year you may find special ticket deals combining the two. This is a fun pool with a climb-on pirates' ship with water cannon, waterfalls, rapids and flumes. There is a bar, restaurant and juice bar and plenty of parking. Prices in 1997 were: Adults: £4.80. Children (4–16): £3.40. Family ticket (two adults and two children): £13.90.Under-fours: free.

HOW TO GET THERE AND WHERE TO PARK
Car: Exit junction 3 of M3 and take A322 to Bracknell until a roundabout shows brown tourist signs to the Look out and Coral Reef pool. Turn left at this roundabout and entrance to the Look out is just 200 yards down this road (B3430). Entrance to the Coral Reef just before. Alternatively take junction 10 off M4 and follow A329(M) for six miles until A322 where follow signs for Bracknell/Bagshot then follow brown galleon signs for Coral Reef. Plentiful free parking within the grounds and a special area reserved for the disabled.

OPENING HOURS
All year, daily, 10 a.m.–5 p.m. (although visits to the Discovery Outpost may be limited to two hours at peak periods).
Closed: Christmas week.

ADMISSION
Adults: £3. Children (5–16): £2. Senior citizens, students, unemployed, disabled: £1.75. Family ticket (two adults and two children or one adult with three children): £8.

WHEELCHAIR AND PUSHCHAIR ACCESS
Excellent facilities with ramps from one level of the Discovery Outpost to another and a lift from the ground floor to upper level. The only area that appeared not to be accessible to wheels was the look-out tower. Many of

the wide-open track walks are certainly negotiable with a pushchair. The coffee shop has a separate wheelchair access from outside by the play area.

REFRESHMENTS

An excellent coffee shop is located to the left of the entrance but it is also accessible from the play area. It serves coffee at 70p, tea at 60p, cappuccino at £1 and a large selection of hot and cold snacks and meals ranging from a bacon roll (£1.80), vegeburger (£1.70), cream tea (£2), a children's meal of sausage and beans (£1), and lots of fresh cakes and sandwiches as well as cartons of juice for 60p and the usual selection of fizzy drinks, crisps and ice-cream. The quarry-tiled room is bright and spacious with room to negotiate pushchairs as well as supplying high-chairs. Wooden animals popped up from behind a wooden frieze around the ceiling and the staff were friendly and efficient. No polystyrene cups here with our hot drinks served in proper mugs. There are six wooden benches outside the café overlooking the play area and a vast area of tables and chairs for picnics adjacent to the play area. The coffee shop is open the same hours as the Discovery Outpost. No food or drink is allowed inside the Discovery Outpost.

SHOP

A small but thoughtful selection of gifts with wooden mini puzzles, John Adams toys, Dorling and Kindersley sticker books, loads of pocket-money toys including pieces of semi-precious minerals for 99p, greetings cards, bath products, oil burners and candles. No cheap tat. Open same hours as Discovery Outpost.

TOILET FACILITIES

Toilets located to the right of the reception area with a separate mother-and-baby room and separate wheelchair toilet. There are further toilets in the café but although both men's and women's have wheelchair access, you are requested not to change nappies in here.

CLOAKROOM

No.

PHOTOGRAPHY

Allowed, but no film sold.

DOGS

Guide dogs only allowed inside. There are tether posts outside and dogs are allowed in the woods with a special dog walk as well.

MADAME TUSSAUD'S AND THE PLANETARIUM

MARYLEBONE ROAD, LONDON, NW1
TEL: 0171 935 6861

HOW LONG SHOULD WE SPEND THERE?
Allow two hours.

WHICH AGE GROUP WILL IT APPEAL TO?
Suitable for all ages.

INTRODUCTION
Madame Tussaud's is something of a London institution due in no small part to the heavy and successful marketing of the name and the children were desperate to go. Firstly, prepare yourself for the queues – we arrived at 11 a.m. on a Sunday and queued for 30 minutes. The line does move reasonably steadily but if you have tetchy children it could be interminable and the wait could be much longer. Think about pre-booking your tickets as this allows you to walk straight in. The museum is divided into the Garden Party, Superstars, Grand Hall, Chamber of Horrors and Spirit of London sections. The figures are variably impressive in their accuracy and many are startlingly lifelike but you'll find that the children simply don't know who many of them are and the simple signs add little. A guidebook at £3.50 promises more information.

The Chamber of Horrors is definitely not for the faint-hearted and even our bloodthirsty pair who were keen to see it were completely overwhelmed by the very realistic figures, the darkness, sounds and smells. I'm sure this reaction depends on your individual children but don't underestimate the gruesomeness – you can take a side exit if it proves too much. By far the biggest highlight is the time-taxi ride called the Spirit of London where you are whisked through a potted history of the capital from early times to modern day using a series of brightly coloured and animated tableaux complete with music and sound effects. The children loved this. All in all, an unusual experience and worth doing at least once. After disembarking from the Spirit of London ride you move seamlessly from Madame Tussaud's to the London Planetarium without leaving the building.

The foyer contains a small exhibition on astronomy and space travel (and a very terrestrial snack shop); the Planetarium show runs continuously through the day and lasts 30 minutes so your longest wait will be half an hour. The seats at the back are best and you simply recline and enjoy the show as the panoply of heavenly bodies is displayed and explained using multi-million pound state-of-the-art projection equipment. The computer-generated journey through space is quite thrilling and the 'preferably no children under-five' notices are not ill-considered; a chattering or crying child will spoil the atmosphere completely and it's a long show for those with short attention spans.

HOW TO GET THERE AND WHERE TO PARK
Car: Meter parking around Regent's Park.
Underground: Two-minute walk from Baker Street station.
Train: Ten-minute walk from Marylebone station.

OPENING HOURS
Madame Tussaud's: All year, daily, 9 a.m.–5.30 p.m. (last admission).
Planetarium: All year, daily, 9 a.m.–5.40 p.m.

ADMISSION
Madame Tussaud's: Adults: £9.25. Children (under-16): £6.10. Senior citizens: £6.95.
Planetarium: Adults: £5.85. Children (under-16): £3.85. Senior citizens: £4.50.
Madame Tussaud's and Planetarium combined ticket: Adults: £11.50. Children (under-16): £7.55. Senior citizens: £8.75. Under-fives: free. Wheelchair users: free. No family ticket.

WHEELCHAIR AND PUSHCHAIR ACCESS
All areas except the Superstars section fully accessible to wheelchairs. Wheelchair users can use the Spirit of London ride only if they enter the

carriages with the help from attendants. Pushchairs are not allowed but baby carriers are available on request.

REFRESHMENTS
The Pier café is a very mediocre establishment serving reasonably priced fast food – pizza slice £1.85, chips £1, vegetarian quiche £1.80, Ciabatta sandwiches £2.20, tea 70p, coffee 85p and soft drinks from 99p. No high-chairs. Give it a miss unless you're desperate but there's nowhere to eat your own food unless you sit on the floor while killing the 30-minute wait for the Planetarium show. There is also a small refreshment stall and vending machines in the Planetarium foyer.

SHOP
An enormous establishment serving both Madame Tussaud's and the Planetarium with a wide range of gifts ranging from truly tacky, plastic Big Ben ornaments to great space books. Good place to stock up on Hallowe'en accessories.

TOILET FACILITIES
Baby-changing facilities at the entrance to the toilets as you exit from the lift before entering the Garden Party and at the end of the exhibition.

CLOAKROOM
By the entrance but for pushchairs only – no bags.

PHOTOGRAPHY
Allowed everywhere except the Chamber of Horrors but no camcorders. Film sold in the shop.

DOGS
Guide dogs only.

MILL GREEN MUSEUM AND MILL

MILL GREEN HAMLET, HERTFORDSHIRE
TEL: 01 707 271362 (WELWYN HATFIELD MUSEUM SERVICE)

HOW LONG SHOULD WE SPEND THERE?
Allow one hour.

WHICH AGE GROUP WILL IT APPEAL TO?
Suitable for age three and upwards.

INTRODUCTION
A small museum but well worth the visit. The main attraction is the fully restored watermill which is best visited at milling time (milling is subject to certain conditions so best to ring first) when, accompanied by the roar of the River Lea as it rushes through the wooden water-wheel, the miller will explain the processes as they happen in front of you. The mill machinery is fully visible with clear text explanations at key points. Afterwards pop into the museum, quaint rather than hi-tech, displaying various items of local history in what used to be the home of the working millers. There are two permanent galleries with Iron Age, Stone Age and Roman finds, old agricultural tools and other local artefacts. By far the most popular exhibit with our kids was the period doll's-house over which the curator is happy to enthuse. Exit through the shop to buy your flour which has been freshly ground from organically grown wheat.

HOW TO GET THERE AND WHERE TO PARK
Car: Leave the A1(M) at junction 3 or 4, then follow the brown signs from

the A1000 or the A414. Free parking is easy in the cul-de-sac road outside (no restrictions).

Train: A 20-minute walk from Hatfield station.

OPENING HOURS
Tuesday to Friday, 10 a.m.–5 p.m. Saturday, Sunday and bank holidays, 2 p.m.–5 p.m. Milling times, Tuesday, Wednesday and Sunday, 2.30 p.m.–4.30 p.m. (subject to change depending on demand for flour and weather conditions).

ADMISSION
Free.

WHEELCHAIR AND PUSHCHAIR ACCESS
There is access to the ground floor but overall it is not good. The mill operates on two levels only accessible by stairs and the museum is housed in small rooms with not much room for manoeuvrability.

REFRESHMENTS
No facilities, but benches outside available in the summer (but not in winter).

SHOP
It is worth popping into the small museum shop first to pick up leaflets and quiz sheet for the older children (small charge). The shop also sells books of local interest, flour ground in the mill and postcards.

TOILET FACILITIES
Unisex toilet available with wheelchair access. No special baby-changing facilities.

CLOAKROOM
No.

PHOTOGRAPHY
Allowed.

DOGS
Not allowed inside but could be safely tethered outside the building.

MOUNTFITCHET CASTLE AND NORMAN VILLAGE

STANSTED, ESSEX

TEL: 01279 813237/0891 424103 (24-HOUR INFORMATION LINE)

HOW LONG SHOULD WE SPEND THERE?
Allow two hours.

WHICH AGE GROUP WILL IT APPEAL TO?
Suitable for all ages.

INTRODUCTION
This is a truly unique attraction as it is the only Norman motte and bailey castle in the world, having been reconstructed on its original site of 1066. Despite this, it is not grand and there is still an amateurish feel about the place in some ways. The site is very hilly so be prepared for much uphill walking. You explore the village, wandering from the gory prison complete with bloodstained victims, to the smithy, a typical dwelling, investigate a bread oven, pottery kiln, church and other constituents of a community designed to be entirely self-sufficient in times of siege. Your path leads eventually to the baron's hall in the inner bailey. Each building has models dressed in period costume as well as the equipment and perhaps food of the time. The signs are good and there is taped information in most of the buildings often as spoken by the supposed inhabitants which helps to bring it all to life. Tame deer, goats and hens wander freely as they would have done in the period and an authentic coracle boat rests by the pond where fresh fish would have been caught for the baron's table. The fortified site is also dotted with Norman weaponry

119

such as a huge catapult and the children can climb the look-out tower.

HOW TO GET THERE AND WHERE TO PARK
Car: Exit junction 8 off M11, then follow signs. Car-parking is plentiful and
   free.
Train: Stansted Mountfitchet station, from Liverpool Street to Cambridge.
   Three-minute walk from the station.

OPENING HOURS
12 March to 12 November, daily, 10 a.m.–5 p.m. (last admission 4 p.m.).

ADMISSION
Adults: £4. Children (3–14): £3. Senior citizens and students: £3.60. No
family ticket.

WHEELCHAIR AND PUSHCHAIR ACCESS
Extremely difficult and not recommended. It is all rough ground and very
steep in places.

REFRESHMENTS
Rather basic environment and fare but the friendly staff compensate.
Sandwiches at £1.50, home-made cakes and hot and cold drinks. No high-
chairs but a reasonable amount of room for buggies. There is a picnic area
just beyond the entrance if you want to take your own food.

SHOP
Disappointing selection of cheap tat with the more rare, worthy items such
as worksheets at 20p. Much of the selection is vaguely historical in theme.

TOILET FACILITIES
Located at the entrance/exit with wheelchair access but no baby-changing
facilities.

CLOAKROOM
No.

PHOTOGRAPHY
Allowed.

DOGS
Guide dogs only because of the loose animals.

MUSEUM OF LONDON

LONDON WALL, LONDON, EC2Y 5HN
TEL: 0171 600 3699   FAX: 0171 600 1056

HOW LONG SHOULD WE SPEND THERE?
Allow three hours.

WHICH AGE GROUP WILL IT APPEAL TO?
Suitable for over-fives.

INTRODUCTION
We had expected a rather dull place and were really surprised by just how interesting this vast museum is. It claims to be the largest, most comprehensive city museum in the world and as I'd be a poor judge of the accuracy of this claim, I have to give it the benefit of the doubt based on our experience. You can follow the unfolding story of the capital from prehistoric times through to the modern day through two floors of fascinating exhibits. There is a wealth of artefacts dredged from the Thames or painstakingly excavated from beneath the modern-day surface of the city, and these have been incorporated into reconstructed Stone Age butchering sites, Roman ruins and much more using sound effects, models and touch databases to set the scene. Subsequent centuries are equally well depicted from Tudor Britain and the Stuarts through to Victorian shop-fronts full of merchandise and it includes the twentieth century. The Lord Mayor's ceremonial coach is also housed here alongside an exhibit of cars.

There is not a huge amount of interactivity but the explanations are excellent, and the reconstructed exhibits are also of a high standard; the only problem could be that the sheer scale of the museum means it could be difficult to hold younger children's attention for the time it takes to get round everything. It would be better to limit your visit to a particular section and since your ticket is valid for three months, perhaps come back and do other areas later. It's worth calling first since there's an extensive events calendar, including those aimed specifically at families – we were treated to a workshop on Victorian childhood and a talk by a Victorian street seller of medicines and spices.

HOW TO GET THERE AND WHERE TO PARK

Car: London Wall car-park, which is right next to the museum, charges just £2 all day on Saturdays, Sundays and bank holidays. Well signposted around the Barbican complex.

Underground: Short walk from Barbican, Bank, St Paul's and Moorgate stations.

Train: Short walk from Moorgate, Liverpool Street, Cannon Street and Farringdon stations.

OPENING HOURS

All year, Tuesday to Saturday, 10 a.m.–5.50 p.m.(last admission 5.30 p.m.). Sunday, 12 noon–5.50 p.m.

Closed: Monday (except bank holidays).

ADMISSION

Adults: £4. Children (5–17): £2. Registered unemployed, students and over-60s: £2. Family ticket (five people, maximum two adults): £9.50. Under-fives: free. Registered disabled and carers: free. All tickets valid for three months.

WHEELCHAIR AND PUSHCHAIR ACCESS

Disabled entrance in Aldersgate Street. Full access to all areas of the museum.

REFRESHMENTS

No facilities actually within the building but there's a pleasant museum café/restaurant opposite the main entrance on the walkway serving quality food, if not cheap. Try Cumberland sausage and mash for £4.95, soup and any sandwich or baguette for £4.20, sandwiches from £1.95, baguettes from £2.50 (roast pork and apple sauce or brie, walnut and grape fillings as well as the more usual). Coffee £1, pot of tea £1.15, cakes from £2, juices £1.20, soft drinks £1. You can eat your picnic in the museum's nursery garden.

SHOP
Extensive shop with a wide variety of books and gifts themed around London.

TOILET FACILITIES
Baby-changing facilities and wheelchair access on the lower level. Wheelchair-access toilet also on the upper (entrance) level.

CLOAKROOM
Supervised cloakroom.

PHOTOGRAPHY
Allowed in the main gallery, but there may be the occasional gallery where photography is not allowed. Film sold.

DOGS
Guide dogs only.

MUSEUM OF THE MOVING IMAGE

SOUTH BANK, WATERLOO, LONDON, SE1 8XT
TEL: 0171 401 2636 (24-HOUR INFORMATION)/0171 815 1350

HOW LONG SHOULD WE SPEND THERE?
Allow at least two hours.

WHICH AGE GROUP WILL IT APPEAL TO?
Suitable for over-fives.

INTRODUCTION
This is an enormous museum on three levels and is excellent value for money with practically every bit of wall space packed with pictures and information; it almost seems as though there is not enough room to show all the exhibits. The museum charts the development of moving images as entertainment from Oriental shadow puppets to modern-day cinema, television and video, touch-screen databases and even a full-scale Odeon cinema. Actors in period costume dramatically bring to life aspects of the film industry; a hugely enthusiastic American casting director in Hollywood brilliantly entices young participants to audition for a part in a dance musical. The signs are good although the descriptions are often quite technical and although there's a fair amount of things to try, the interactive area is centred primarily in one place where you can draw your own picture strip for a zoetrope, record an interview with Barry Norman, be a newscaster or fly over London. There is a small toddlers' play area but on the whole you have to be older to fully appreciate what's on offer. Other nice touches are the glass-fronted working projection room of the 1930s cinema. There's a guidebook available for £2.95 and a programme of activities in the workshop.

HOW TO GET THERE AND WHERE TO PARK

Car: Head for Upper Ground – a street adjacent to the South Bank complex – where you'll find meter parking and an NCP car-park. Visitors arriving between 10 a.m. and 5 p.m. qualify for reduced parking prices if they have their tickets stamped at the museum ticket desk.

Underground: A five-minute walk from Waterloo (South Bank exit) and also from Embankment (cross Hungerford Bridge to the South Bank).

Train: As above.

OPENING HOURS

All year, daily, 10 a.m.–6 p.m. (last admission 5.30 p.m.).
Closed: 24–26 December.

ADMISSION

Adults: £6.25. Children (5–16) and concessions: £4.50. Students: £5.25. Wheelchair users: £4.50. Carers and under-fives: free.

WHEELCHAIR AND PUSHCHAIR ACCESS

Almost all areas of the museum are accessible to wheels. Where there are stairs there are help-point telephones from which you can call for assistance on the stair lifts or regular lifts. Only the documentary newsreel and Russian train exhibits cannot be accessed by wheelchairs. The Film café can be reached with help via a short detour outside. The shop is not fully accessible to wheelchairs.

REFRESHMENTS

The South Bank complex has a bar and the new, licensed Film café opened recently serving a variety of food, both hot and cold. Own food is best eaten on the benches outside overlooking the Thames.

SHOP

A huge shop which is open from 10.30 a.m. to 6.30 p.m. with a wide selection of postcards, greetings cards, film posters, all sorts of paraphernalia related to cinema and TV and MOMI-branded merchandise such as bags and caps. Lots of grown-up books and interesting gifts such as zoetropes.

TOILET FACILITIES

At the entrance only. Wheelchair-access and pull-down baby-changing table in the ladies'.

CLOAKROOM
Only pushchairs can be stored for security reasons.

PHOTOGRAPHY
Allowed.

DOGS
Guide dogs only.

THE NATIONAL GALLERY

TRAFALGAR SQUARE, LONDON, WC2N 5DN
TEL: 0171 839 3321

HOW LONG SHOULD WE SPEND THERE?
Allow two hours.

WHICH AGE GROUP WILL IT APPEAL TO?
Particularly suitable for six years and upwards, but all ages would get something out of the day. However, it is the sort of place where a screaming baby would be very conspicuous!

INTRODUCTION
We had been planning a Christmas day out in town to join the masses gazing longingly in Hamley's windows and decided to combine it with a visit to the National Gallery.

Viewing the 2,000 pictures from the thirteenth to the early twentieth centuries would have been too much for us – let alone the children – but a very helpful information desk provided us with a children's quiz book cleverly produced and illustrated by none other than Quentin Blake. This involved 'hunt the painting' (with thankfully some tips on which gallery to head for!) and then answering questions about what they could see in the pictures and drawing space for some of their own. A most painless introduction to a national cultural institution and it proved a huge success with our six- and nine-year-olds. An hour flew by looking selectively at Rousseau, Hogarth, a beautiful Dutch peepshow box, Holbein and many others. Such an imaginative approach in introducing children to serious art will certainly encourage many future visits and, with free admission, this is undoubtedly excellent value for money and ideal for a wet weekend.

During the holidays watch out for a programme of talks aimed at a young audience where the children are invited to sit on a Magic Carpet in front of a particular painting while a speaker explains in child-friendly language all about it (rather edifying for adults too!). There are extras available such as a portable CD player with commentary on over 1,000 paintings. There is also a highlights tour.

HOW TO GET THERE AND WHERE TO PARK

Car: Parking in central London is a nightmare. There is a large car-park in Whitcombe Street behind the gallery, but it's not cheap.

Underground: Charing Cross station is a five-minute walk or Leicester Square station a ten-minute walk.

Train: Charing Cross station is a five-minute walk.

OPENING HOURS

All year, Monday, Tuesday, Thursday, Friday and Saturday, 10 a.m.–6 p.m. Wednesday, 10 a.m.–8 p.m. Sunday, 12 noon–6 p.m.
Closed: 1 January, Good Friday, 24–26 December.

ADMISSION

Free.

WHEELCHAIR AND PUSHCHAIR ACCESS

Excellent, wide doorways and no stairs that cannot be circumvented by the lift. Make sure you enter by the Sainsbury wing or Orange Street entrance where you can gain immediate access to the lift to take you to all floors.

REFRESHMENTS

There is an upmarket brasserie in the Sainsbury wing with waitress service and an imaginative menu with prices from £2.95 for afternoon tea to £12.95 for a two-course lunch. (Minimum charge £6 per person between 11.45 a.m. and 2.30 p.m.) Open daily until 5 p.m. the basement café in the main building is a Prêt a Manger franchise and so serves reliable, good quality fresh food, if a little pricey. The facilities were spacious, seating plentiful and high-chairs available, but the café is self-service so the usual problems arise if you are a lone adult impersonating a pack horse. Newspapers available if you have the time and inclination! Open 10 a.m. to 5 p.m. own food not allowed. Both restaurants are licensed.

SHOP

The main shop is on the ground floor of the Sainsbury wing and as you might expect, is very upmarket compared to most equivalent establish-ments and no 'rubbish' in sight! Our children settled on mini-prints of paintings they had seen during the quiz at £3.95 each but they could have gone for poster size ones at £10. Some beautiful coffee table and educational books including many aimed at children (Eye Witness series), CD-roms, jigsaws, notebooks, T-shirts and small items within a pocket-money budget. The shop opens at the same time as the museum until 30 minutes before museum closing time. There is also a smaller shop in Room 3 of the main building.

TOILET FACILITIES
Located on the first floor and lower ground floor. There are baby-changing facilities in one set of toilets in both the Sainsbury wing (lower ground) and main building (lower floor). However, those in the Sainsbury wing were kept locked so you need a nearby warder for access as with the disabled toilets. All toilets have wheelchair access.

CLOAKROOM
Free cloakroom but will only take clothing.

PHOTOGRAPHY
Not allowed in the gallery but splendid views of Trafalgar Square and Big Ben in the distance from the entrance so worth taking a camera along.

DOGS
Guide dogs only.

NATIONAL MARITIME MUSEUM

ROMNEY ROAD, GREENWICH, LONDON, SE10 9NF
TEL: 0181 858 4422/0181 312 6565 (RECORDED INFORMATION)
FAX: 0181 312 6632

HOW LONG SHOULD WE SPEND THERE?
Allow two hours for the museum itself.

WHICH AGE GROUP WILL IT APPEAL TO?
Suitable for all ages, but younger children may find it hard going until they reach the All Hands Gallery.

INTRODUCTION
The museum consists of a main gallery dominated by the quarter size skeleton of a huge ship into which are set the various themed exhibitions covering multifarious aspects of sea trade and sea warfare. These include: an impressive hands-on ship's operations room which the children loved and a video wall with random images of twentieth-century sea power. All well done but the Nelson exhibition is truly excellent in every way, from the exhibits themselves to the last detail – including the lighting and sound. The context is set with historical background, details of Nelson's early life, his marriage and subsequent affair with Emma Hamilton, his many wartime achievements and of course the famous Battle of Trafalgar where he died. As well as the usual text boards there are clever 'rollers', novel devices which, when turned, reveal another piece of information. There is of course video, including an animated reconstruction of the battle and an impressive display of the very bloodstained uniform Nelson

was wearing when fatally wounded. If the younger children are getting restless, the upper floor takes you to the All Hands Gallery which gets full marks for ingenuity and will delight most children up to ten and many adults too. This is a wonderful place for children with exhibits in clever child-safe boxes carefully crafted to resemble ship's cargo, each one with questions on the outside inviting you to look inside and find the answers. There's a crane you can operate to load up a ship; you can feel what it's like to manipulate the robot hands of a pressurised diving suit, or fire a cannon at a computerised target. A wonderful place. There are plenty of holiday activities too, so ask for a leaflet at reception or call the recorded information line. Greenwich itself makes a vibrant destination with its markets and shops.

HOW TO GET THERE AND WHERE TO PARK

Car: Connections from the M25 via the A2 or A13/A102 Blackwall tunnel. The museum is located off Jamaica Road (A200). Pay-and-display parking is available beyond the Naval College travelling towards Maze Hill railway station and there is also parking above the Royal Observatory (but a long steep walk thereafter).

Train: Greenwich or Maze Hill is less than 20 minutes from Charing Cross. You can also travel on the Docklands Light Railway to Island Gardens and connect to Greenwich via the foot tunnel under the Thames – an experience in itself. The lift from the tunnel brings you out at the Cutty Sark.

Boat: River cruises run from Westminster, Charing Cross and Tower piers.

OPENING HOURS

All year, daily, 10 a.m.–5 p.m.
Closed: 24–26 December.

ADMISSION

Adults: £5.50. Children (5–16): £3. Concessions: £4.50. Family ticket (two children and two adults): £16. The ticket allows for entry to the museum and the Queen's House and the Old Royal Observatory, both of which are located within walking distance, and with one free return visit within a year of purchase.

WHEELCHAIR AND PUSHCHAIR ACCESS

Excellent – with a small lift to negotiate the steps at the entrance, a lift for access to all floors and wide, spacious gangways.

REFRESHMENTS

The large and licensed Bosun's café serves morning coffee and hot meals from £3.65, with a children's menu with prices starting at £2.50. There is a selection of cakes and scones from 65p. Tea and coffee 75p, with soft drinks from 95p. Although reasonably priced, the food was uninspiring and had a mass-produced look. There are additional tables outside but no facilities for eating your own food although Greenwich park, in which the museum is situated, offers a perfect picnic site in fine weather. We spotted three high-chairs. Alternatively, lively Greenwich is full of cafés, restaurants and pubs that serve a wide selection of food.

SHOP

Located by the entrance/exit and stocked with all sorts of goodies from 'English' toiletries to videos, CDs, jewellery, jams and gift-wrapped chocolates. There are also pocket-money toys, such as wooden boats and puzzles. A wide and tempting selection.

TOILET FACILITIES

Stairs and a lift access the toilets in the basement. There is a baby-changing facility and wheelchair-access toilet, but in the same room.

CLOAKROOM

Locked cloakroom.

PHOTOGRAPHY

Not allowed.

DOGS

Guide dogs only.

NATURAL HISTORY MUSEUM

CROMWELL ROAD, LONDON, SW7 5BD
TEL: 0171 938 9123   FAX: 0171 938 9155

HOW LONG SHOULD WE SPEND THERE?
Allow at least two hours.

WHICH AGE GROUP WILL IT APPEAL TO?
Suitable for all ages.

INTRODUCTION
There are two main sections to the museum: the Life Galleries housed in the old Victorian building (which is quite something in itself, but whose charms are likely to be lost on the younger members of the family), entered via Cromwell Road, and the more recently established Earth Galleries, entered from Exhibition Road.

We started in the Life Galleries and with the help of a map and information sheets (30p each) from the information desk in the entrance hall we explored the ground-floor galleries, including those about birds, marine life and mammals. The latter consists of a room packed with models, many suspended from the ceiling. Although there are a few interactive displays around the perimeter, many were not working and the room seemed in need of a bit of rejuvenation compared to many others in the museum. The children did, however, enjoy comparing their weight on some special scales to that of a blue whale and other mammals. The adults in the party did not indulge in this for fear of an unfavourable comparison. These are interesting but unspectacular next to the fabulous dinosaur exhibition which is colossal in every way. Toddlers will have to be lifted up to see the animatronics dinosaur fight with sound effects, and the detailed exhibition afterwards may not interest them but will fascinate the older members of the party.

The other gallery in this section of the museum, which will hold just about everyone's attention, is devoted to human biology. This is very interactive and entices you to play games about genetics and other aspects of the body and you can watch a video which uses graphics to show human reproduction. It's highly educational as well as entertaining. Another gallery guaranteed to provoke a response if not always a vote of approval is creepy-crawlies. There is lots of movement in this one and I defy you not to scratch. You can walk through the Ecology section with a strong slant on conservation on the way to the Earth Galleries. Amongst other interesting displays is one that shows the death and decay of a rabbit – not as grisly as it sounds but sufficiently so to command attention.

The Earth Galleries consist of a ground floor of static but large and imposing exhibits on the earth's history, before you then move upstairs via an escalator which cleverly takes you through the middle of a huge earth sculpture. On the first floor they are preparing for the two new permanent exhibitions on the story of the earth's formation and the earth's treasury – a display of minerals and gemstones scheduled to open in 1998. The second floor is still very much alive and kicking – especially where you can experience an earthquake and see the effects of other natural phenomena graphically illustrated. Also there's masses of interactivity in the Restless Surface section, where you can see how the elements and other natural forces as well as living things shape our planet. Much of it went over our children's heads but there's certainly enough for even the younger ones to go away having been entertained and, hopefully, having learnt more about the world.

You can join highlight tours which can be booked at the Life Galleries information desk and which run every hour from 11 a.m. to 4 p.m. and there are tours for the Wildlife Garden twice a day during May to September.

HOW TO GET THERE AND WHERE TO PARK

Car: Car-park in Imperial College Road or on-street meter parking. Several bays for disabled vehicles outside the Exhibition Road entrance.

Underground: South Kensington station has an exit in Exhibition Road, only a few minutes' walk from the museum.

Train: Victoria station then take the underground.

OPENING HOURS

All year, Monday to Saturday, 10 a.m.–5.50 p.m. Sunday, 11 a.m.–5.50 p.m. Closed: 23–26 December.

ADMISSION

Natural History Museum only: Adults: £6. Children (5–17): £3.99. Senior citizens and wheelchair users (carers free): £3.20. Family ticket (two adults and four children): £16.

Natural History Museum, Science Museum and the Victoria and Albert Museum: Adults: £21. Children (5–17): £11. Concessions: £11. Family ticket (two adults and four children): £43.

Entry is free after 4.30 p.m. Monday to Friday and after 5 p.m. Saturday, Sunday and bank holidays.

WHEELCHAIR AND PUSHCHAIR ACCESS

Full access with lifts to all floors. Best for wheelchair users to go to the Exhibition Road entrance which has a couple of steps; if these can't be negotiated there is a rear entrance in Museum Lane where staff will assist.

REFRESHMENTS

The Waterhouse café on the ground floor is a Prue Leith establishment and serves a small selection of sandwiches, pastries and cakes. Soft drinks cost from 95p, pastries £1.25, sandwiches from £1.75, coffee £1, tea £1 per pot. The Gallery restaurant is open 10 a.m. to 11 a.m. for morning coffee and serving lunch from 11.30 a.m. to 2.30 p.m. Afternoon tea is available from 3.30 p.m. to 5 p.m. A typical selection from the menu would be mushroom and lentil soup at £2.50 and poached salmon in lemon sauce for £4.95. There's also a more subdued children's menu and, even better, child-sized portions of the adult menu for £2.50 (why don't more establishments do this?). There are two high-chairs. You'll find the Globe café in the Earth Galleries section of the museum which serves light snacks and there's a snack bar in the Life Galleries basement where you'll also find the picnic area – open at weekends and in the school holidays only.

SHOP

There's a large gift shop off Waterhouse Way between the Life and Earth Galleries stocking toys, sweets, toiletries, greetings cards, postcards, T-shirts, posters, puzzles, games, lots of dinosaurs and a plethora of museum-related goods. There is also a separate bookshop here with a large selection of both specialised and great kids' books. The Earth store in the Earth Galleries section of the museum concentrates more on minerals such as chunks of rock as well as stocking cards, posters, books and games; smaller but useful for more specialised gifts.

TOILET FACILITIES

Disabled toilets on ground and basement levels of Life Galleries. Baby-changing and feeding room on ground level of Life Galleries and also on the upper levels of Earth Galleries.

CLOAKROOM

On the upper level of Life Galleries and the upper level of Earth Galleries. Pushchairs can be left and free baby carriers available.

PHOTOGRAPHY

Not allowed.

DOGS

Guide dogs only.

ODDS FARM PARK

WOODBURN COMMON, HIGH WYCOMBE, BUCKINGHAMSHIRE, HP10 0LG
TEL: 01628 520188

HOW LONG SHOULD WE SPEND THERE?
Allow two hours.

WHICH AGE GROUP WILL IT APPEAL TO?
Suitable for all ages.

INTRODUCTION
There's a really friendly feel to this well-tended farm which is also a Rare
Breeds Survival Trust approved centre. A great deal of effort has been
made to make everything as child-friendly as possible, and it shows. There
are daily activities such as bottle-feeding the lambs or calves, collecting
eggs, sometimes face painting and a variety of additional weekend events.
Pick up a 30p bag of feed at the entrance so that you can feed the many
unusual breeds of goats, sheep, pigs, hens, Highland cattle, ponies and pets
corner. Most of the pens have signs with explanations of the breeds but not
all have the child-friendly versions which are good for the younger ones
unable to digest all the data. There are two excellent outdoor play areas
with good wooden apparatus, a special under-fives closed section and
sandpits with lots of toys. There's also a huge barn filled with bales of hay
for active play and many sit-on toys and tyres. Tables and benches have
been thoughtfully placed in this area so you can oversee the proceedings.
The grounds are quite large so you can choose to take a 20-minute tractor-
driven trailer ride around the paddocks, but the children will appreciate
getting closer to the animals if you walk.

HOW TO GET THERE AND WHERE TO PARK
Car: Exit at junction 7 of the M4 following A355 to Slough and

137

Beaconsfield or take the exit at junction 2 of the M40 and head towards Burnham Beeches picking up the brown 'bull's head' tourist signs. Limited free parking on site.

Train: To Beaconsfield station from Marylebone then a £5 taxi ride to the farm. No bus service.

OPENING HOURS

February half-term to mid-September, Thursday to Sunday inclusive, 10 a.m.–5 p.m.

Mid-September to February half-term, Thursday to Sunday inclusive, 10 a.m.–4 p.m.

Closed: 1–2 January, 25–26 December.

ADMISSION

Adults: £3.50. Children (over two): £2.25. Senior citizens: £2.50. Special-needs adults and helpers: £2. Special-needs children: £1.50. There are lots of promotional days with special offers so ring for details.

WHEELCHAIR AND PUSHCHAIR ACCESS

Good if you can handle wheels over grassy terrain but no wheelchairs or pushchairs allowed in the tea room.

REFRESHMENTS

The tea room serves cakes from 50p, clotted cream tea for £1.90, salads at £2.50, beefburgers at £1.60 and tea for 70p. They also have a children's menu (hot-dogs, spaghetti on toast) for £1.20 and picnic boxes for £1.95, as well as the usual selection of crisps and sweets. There's plenty of room but no wheelchairs or pushchairs are allowed. High-chairs available. Games, crayons and paper on the tables were a nice touch. You can't eat your own food inside but head for the barn or the various picnic areas around the farm and play areas.

SHOP

Small, but quality feel, with beeswax products from the farm, farm toys and animals, furry toys, mugs, chutneys, jams and biscuits, posters and gift cards all with farm or animal themes.

TOILET FACILITIES

Separate baby-changing facilities. There's a separate wheelchair-access toilet and a child step, child toilet seat and child-height wash-basin were thoughtful touches in the ladies' toilets.

CLOAKROOM
No.

PHOTOGRAPHY
Allowed but no film sold.

DOGS
Guide dogs only.

PARADISE WILDLIFE PARK

WHITE STUBBS LANE, BROXBOURNE, HERTS, EN10 7QA
TEL: 01992 468001 (RECORDED MESSAGE)/01992 470490
FAX: 01992 440525

HOW LONG SHOULD WE SPEND THERE?
Allow two to three hours.

WHICH AGE GROUP WILL IT APPEAL TO?
Suitable for all ages.

INTRODUCTION
What you might call an honest sort of place with no trace of sophistication but a lot of earnest enthusiasts. Set in Broxbourne woods and leisure park and billing itself as Britain's most interactive wildlife park, the real attractions are the animals – ranging from the rabbits and donkeys to the lions and tigers. There is a daily programme of animal encounters and feeding times with certain animals. Camels and zebras vied for attention along with reptiles and birds, but were really no contest for the tigers (the closest we had been to the real thing in our visits to various other wildlife centres). You can have photo-sessions with the tigers for a considerable extra charge and actually play with the baby tiger for about 20 minutes or so. Pots of food could be bought at 25p to give to the more accessible animals which helped to give the air of being involved. Attempts at mini-themed playgrounds are less successful, the Fantasy Land consisting of an old fire engine, some Wendy houses and a miniature fun fair was hardly impressive, but the woodland railway and play area are lots of fun and nicely done. Rides on a little van, crazy golf, tractor-trailer and pony rides were available around the site but all these cost a little extra at 50p each

and expenses can soon mount up. The park has been going for over ten years and has an active scheme concerned with raising money to protect wild animals in Africa. The animals seemed healthy and the children loved it. Take a walk in the park afterwards. A fair-weather activity.

HOW TO GET THERE AND WHERE TO PARK

Car: Signposted off the A10 at the Turnford and Wormley junction. Parking is plentiful within the park itself.

Train: A courtesy bus will pick you up from Broxbourne station. Simply ask at the ticket office upon arrival and they will call the park.

OPENING HOURS

Summer, daily, 10 a.m.–6 p.m.
Winter, daily, 10 a.m.–dusk.

ADMISSION

Adults: £5. Children (3–15) and senior citizens: £4. Under-threes: free. No family ticket.

WHEELCHAIR AND PUSHCHAIR ACCESS

This is ideal territory for wheels as everything is on the flat.

REFRESHMENTS

There is a bar for the diehards, a restaurant near the entrance, an open-air snack bar with outdoor seating and a self-service café. The café serves average-looking hot and cold snacks (sandwiches £1.50, baked potatoes £1.95 to £2.75, hot-dogs, scones, cakes), and on the day we visited it was packed with visitors and accompanying buggies, principally because there appeared to be no high-chairs available – an odd omission. There are plenty of picnic tables outside the café and around the park and an undercover picnic area in Jungle Theatre.

SHOP

Not very inspiring, with a large selection of cheap gifts

TOILET FACILITIES

Wheelchair access and baby-changing facilities.

CLOAKROOM

None but helpful staff find somewhere to help you stow things if necessary.

PHOTOGRAPHY
No restrictions and film sold.

DOGS
Not allowed in the animal section but can be taken into the park.

THE RAGGED SCHOOL MUSEUM

46-50 COPPERFIELD ROAD, LONDON, E3 4RR
TEL: 0181 980 6405

HOW LONG SHOULD WE SPEND THERE?
Allow about one hour.

WHICH AGE GROUP WILL IT APPEAL TO?
Suitable for over-fives.

INTRODUCTION
The museum has been created from a derelict Victorian warehouse and it has been partly restored to its original purpose as part of a Ragged [free] School; in fact it was once the largest such school in London and, between 1877 and 1908, it occupied several buildings along Copperfield Road. These schools were establishments set up in the late nineteenth century by Dr Barnado to educate the poorest of East London's children. Driven by missionary zeal he gave thousands of children a free education and free meals at a time when many Londoners were living in abject poverty in appalling conditions. Sometimes a whole family existed in a single room where they lived, ate, slept, cooked and worked. Often a mother and her children would eke out a meagre existence by doing such work as making matchboxes or putting the bristles in brushes. They would work long hours for a pittance, and they would constantly be at risk from diseases such as typhoid and cholera which were common at the time. The Ragged Schools helped these children from infancy through to their first job with lessons being held in classrooms containing 100 or so children and there were evening classes for the older children.

The museum includes a Victorian classroom where you can sit at the original desks and write on slates; next to the classroom is a large activity area where children's workshops are regularly held. Other activities range from Victorian parlour games to experiencing a Victorian gruel lunch or school lesson. Two other floors of the museum are used for displays on aspects of East End life in Victorian times and information about Dr Barnado's life and work. In fact the museum owns a wealth of artefacts which they are unable to display as they can't yet afford to refurbish the other buildings that they own in Copperfield Street and which were part of the original Ragged School. The museum's ambition, however, is to eventually open all the buildings. This will make it more accessible to all, the activities and displays could be expanded and the opening hours could be extended – all of which is dependent on their Centenary Buildings Appeal. Although this is a small museum and barely qualifies as a full day out, it is well worth a visit especially on a day when there is a children's workshop. An added bonus is that the friendly volunteer staff are only too happy to chat and provide information on any aspect of the museum and its history.

HOW TO GET THERE AND WHERE TO PARK
Car: Take Stepney Green Road right off Mile End Road, follow it into Ben Johnson Road and then second right into Copperfield Road. There is no car-park, but there is meter parking outside and you can park on the yellow lines at weekends. The museum is also signposted off Burdett Road.
Underground: A 15-minute walk from Stepney Green and Mile End stations (both Central line). Signposted across Mile End Park.
Train: To Limehouse via overground or Docklands Light Railway then a ten-minute walk up Aston Street.

OPENING HOURS
All year, Wednesdays and Thursdays, 10 a.m.–5 p.m. *and* the first Sunday of every month, 2 p.m.–5 p.m.

ADMISSION
Free, but donations are welcome.

WHEELCHAIR AND PUSHCHAIR ACCESS
This is a Victorian building with steep, narrow stairs and no lift so there is no wheelchair access and pushchairs are not recommended.

REFRESHMENTS
There is a small café on site on the lower-ground floor overlooking the

canal. It serves a limited range of inexpensive food and drinks – tea at 40p, coffee at 50p, soup at 40p, as well as sweets and crisps. There are a limited number of seats and no highchairs. If you want to bring a picnic you could take it into the park across the road, although this didn't look like a very inviting prospect.

SHOP
There is a small shop to the left of the entrance which sells a range of traditional wooden toys. They also have many pocket-money toys such as balsa-wood gliders and bookmarks – all for less than £1. There are postcards and posters, books on Victorian times and the East End and one or two children's history books.

TOILET FACILITIES
These are found on the lower-ground floor. There is no wheelchair access or baby-changing facilities.

CLOAKROOM
No, but the friendly staff will help by storing things in the shop.

PHOTOGRAPHY
Allowed throughout the museum but no film is sold.

DOGS
Guide dogs only.

THE ROYAL AIR FORCE MUSEUM

GRAHAME PARK WAY, LONDON, NW9 5LL
TEL: 0181 205 9191 (24-HOUR INFORMATION LINE)/0181 205 2266

HOW LONG SHOULD WE SPEND THERE?
Allow one to two hours.

WHICH AGE GROUP WILL IT APPEAL TO?
Suitable for all ages.

INTRODUCTION
The museum consists of two vast sites: the first comprises the main aircraft hall and Bomber Command hall as well as the ticket office, shop, art gallery, 2000 exhibition and the main aircraft. The second site, the Battle of Britain hall, is located across the car-park and provides an insight (if a rather partisan one) into World War II and it would be especially of interest for older children.

Even to the uninitiated, the first site, which incorporates displays of immaculate fighter planes – from the earliest models of World War I to the huge Harrier jump jet – are spectacular and judging by the number of children there on each occasion we have visited, the museum seems to be a perennial favourite. There are plentiful boards and signs with a wealth of technical information for the cognoscenti but if you don't have the time – or the inclination – to absorb all this, you can simply wander between the magnificent flying machines and marvel at the ingenuity of man at war.

The flight simulator is a key attraction but not recommended for children under five, as the Red Arrows and Tornado flight or World War I dog-fight can be very realistic and liable to churn up the most hardened stomach; but at £1.50 it's very good value. You can also examine the cockpit of a Lockheed Tristar with a push-button operated, light-up control panel and you can climb aboard a Jet Provost and take hold of the controls. In the Bomber Command hall there is a special display commemorating Barnes Wallis and his bouncing bomb. As well as a video on the subject, older children can have a go at lining up the gunsights on an imaginary dam.

The upper galley in the main hall is dedicated to World War I artefacts, displays and the art gallery. You can look into the 2000 exhibition on the way out, but we found this disappointing and basically a glorified recruitment drive, while the video on the Euro-Fighter seemed to be simply an advertisement for a piece of wartime hardware. In the Battle of Britain hall the signs and animated displays (with a bombsite reconstruction cleverly animated with a hologram) set the scene before you enter the main aircraft displays while a large video graphically describes the main events of the air battle itself. A display of smaller items is tucked away inside a bomb-shelter tunnel, and upstairs you can find uniforms, an animated display using holograms of a Churchill speech and direct access into a Sunderland flying boat, where a tape talks you through each section of the plane. There are various push-button videos dotted around but, on the whole, the museum is not hugely interactive but impresses by its sheer scale and occasional inventiveness. Guidebook costs £2.25 and guided tours are also available.

HOW TO GET THERE AND WHERE TO PARK

Car: Off A41 into Aerodrome Road (not signposted for the museum) then right into Grahame Park Way. Or off A5 Edgware Road into Colindale Avenue then into Grahame Park Way. Plentiful free car-parking on site.

Underground: A five-minute walk from Colindale station.

Train: Mill Hill Broadway nearest station but a 20-minute walk.

OPENING HOURS

All year, daily, 10 a.m.–6 p.m. (last admission 5.30 p.m.).

ADMISSION

Adults: £5.70. Children (5–16): £2.85. Senior citizens: £4.30. Students and unemployed: £2.85. Under-fives: free. Family ticket (two adults and two children): £13.85. You may also visit a second time for free if you return within six months and you can produce the original ticket.

WHEELCHAIR AND PUSHCHAIR ACCESS
On the whole access is good with spacious aisles between exhibits, however, the lift to the upper floor is situated in the foyer of the main hall and has to be operated by an attendant. There is also a lift to the upper floor of the Battle of Britain hall.

REFRESHMENTS
The Wings restaurant has the air of a function room and rather lacks atmosphere. Having said that, there is a large choice of basic counter-service fare with a cup of tea at 80p, fruit juice at £1, soup and a roll at £1.80, a kid's meal at £2.35 and sandwiches from £1.25. If you wanted something more substantial, vegetable lasagne was on offer at £4.65, as well as various other hot meals. A serious omission was the lack of provision of high-chairs; there is only one for the entire restaurant. Eating your own food is not permitted inside but there is a picnic area outside with around ten tables and one or two benches near the main entrance. The restaurant is open between 10 a.m. and 5 p.m.

SHOP
The shop is large and entirely dedicated to aviation-related merchandise; from leather flying jackets to models, books, jigsaws and all sorts of pocket-money toys. It is open from 10 a.m. to 5 p.m.

TOILET FACILITIES
The toilets are located in the main building with the men's on the ground floor and – annoyingly – the women's and the separate mother-and-baby room on the upper floor which is only accessible by stairs or attendant-operated lift. Supposedly, you needed a key for the mother-and-baby room, but it was unlocked on our visit. Wheelchair access. More toilets can be found in the middle of the main hall, but there are no baby-changing facilities here. There are toilets with a separate wheelchair-access toilet and a mother-and-baby room adjacent to the Wings restaurant and accessible from the Battle of Britain hall.

CLOAKROOM
Supervised cloakroom.

PHOTOGRAPHY
Allowed and they even recommend what sort of film to use and film is sold in the shop.

DOGS
Guide dogs only.

THE ROYAL OBSERVATORY

GREENWICH, LONDON
TEL: 0181 312 6565 (RECORDED INFORMATION)/0181 858 4422
FAX: 0181 312 6632

HOW LONG SHOULD WE SPEND THERE?
Allow one hour.

WHICH AGE GROUP WILL IT APPEAL TO?
Suitable for over-fives.

INTRODUCTION
At the home of Greenwich Mean Time and zero longitude, the Old Observatory has been turned into an interesting exhibition that tells the story of time-keeping, astronomy and the importance of the discovery of zero longitude for navigation at sea. Pick up a guidebook for £2.50 at reception, however, there is no specific children's guide. The main attraction is undoubtedly the prime meridian line itself bedded into a cobbled courtyard where, on a busy day, you will struggle through the hordes of tourists being photographed astride this famous line. It is now enhanced by a clock counting down the seconds to the millennium and you can even have a certificate for £1 showing at exactly what time you stood there. You will also see the red time ball on the roof which rises and drops at 1 p.m. every day. Peep inside the Camera Obscura to experience a 17th-century form of moving entertainment where, in a darkened room, clever use of mirrors allows you to see a picture of Greenwich reflected onto a revolving table. In Flamstead House you can follow the story of the search for the accurate measurement of the illusive longitude; and you can visit the Octagon room used to observe the heavens – the interior of which is a fine

example of Sir Christopher Wren's work. Downstairs there is a special exhibition of time and how the development of an accurate time-keeping device affected seafarers. The Meridian building leads you to the largest refracting telescope in Britain; and there is also a weekday planetarium.

There are some hands-on activities but on the whole the economically laid-out exhibits are often quite technical and older children will appreciate them more. Don't forget that a combined ticket allows you to visit the National Maritime Museum and the Queen's House – although we would not recommend a visit to the Queen's House for children. The Maritime Museum park has a good play area for kids and the lawn area between the museum and the Queen's House hosts a 'summer shipmates' family activity tent with a programme of painting, singing and storytelling so it's worth the walk to the bottom of the hill.

HOW TO GET THERE AND WHERE TO PARK
Car: The centre of Greenwich is horrendous to negotiate especially at weekends. There are car-parks on the A200 near the *Cutty Sark* and next to the Naval College, but I recommend that you park in Charlton Way, off Black Heath.

Boat: Take the boat from Charing Cross and Westminster piers to Greenwich pier. The Observatory is a 35-minute walk from here, with the added attraction of passing the Cutty Sark on the way.

Train: Take the overground from London Bridge or Waterloo to Greenwich or Maze Hill. The Observatory is a 30-minute walk from Greenwich station; a little further from Maze Hill.

OPENING HOURS
All year, daily, 10 a.m.–5 p.m. (last admission 30 minutes before closing). Closed: 24–26 December.

ADMISSION
Combined ticket (allowing access to the National Maritime Museum and the Queen's House as well): Adults: £5.50. Children (5–16): £3. Concessions (students, senior citizens and unemployed): £4.50. Family ticket (two adults and up to three children): £16. Under-fives: free.
The Royal Observatory only: Adults: £4. Children (5–16): £2. Concessions (students, senior citizens and unemployed): £3. Family ticket (two adults and up to three children): £12. Under-fives: free.

WHEELCHAIR AND PUSHCHAIR ACCESS
Only partially accessible to wheelchairs and difficult to negotiate with a

pushchair, some parts being impossible with wheels, although entry to the courtyard to see the Meridian line is possible. If you want to go through the park to the National Maritime Museum at the bottom, you'll have to take the long way round, as the steep, short route is by a long flight of steps.

REFRESHMENTS

No refreshment facilities in the Observatory itself, but there is the Greenwich Park café close by on the main road leading to the Observatory from Charlton Walk which serves a selection of interesting pastries for around £1.50, fresh salads and sandwiches from £1.60, tea at 60p, coffee at 70p and canned drinks from 85p. The ice-cream isn't bad either. You won't find *haute cuisine* but it is definitely a step up from your regular park café with plenty of seating inside and out, although we didn't spot any high-chairs. Alternatively you can eat at the Bosun's café in the Maritime Museum or – better still – have a picnic in the park on a fine day and simply enjoy the space.

SHOP

The shop is small, horribly crowded but with an interesting selection of things like children's telescopes, globes, binoculars, galaxy guides and Dorling and Kindersley books as well as upmarket adult gifts.

TOILET FACILITIES

The combined wheelchair toilet and baby-changing facilities are kept locked. You will have to find an attendant to unlock them and the only toilet we found was in a room accessed by stairs!

CLOAKROOM

Staff at the information desk will help with the storage of any items.

PHOTOGRAPHY

Only allowed in the courtyard.

DOGS

Guide dogs only.

SCIENCE MUSEUM

EXHIBITION ROAD, LONDON, SW7 2DD
TEL: 0171 938 8008/8080/8000
WEB-SITE: HTTP://WWW.NMSI.AC.UK

HOW LONG SHOULD WE SPEND THERE?
Allow anything from two hours to a full day.

WHICH AGE GROUP WILL IT APPEAL TO?
Suitable for all ages.

INTRODUCTION
It would be difficult to praise the Science Museum highly enough. Through the exciting use of every conceivable form of technological innovation this museum now contains many galleries which are the yardstick by which all other large museums should measure themselves. Undoubtedly funding plays a part in all this and the Science Museum does have a big advantage over other museums in terms of attracting corporate sponsorship. From the moment you enter the building the amount of thought that has gone into the place is apparent; the foyer contains a cash dispenser, *bureau de change* and a post office. Also, there is a bank of cash desks to speed you into the museum – including a fast-track till. On the wall is a list of improvements requested by members of the public and next to each one is the way in which the museum has taken these on board.

The museum has five main, wholly interactive galleries: Launch Pad, Flight Lab, The Garden, Things and On Air. The Garden and Things are located in the newly redeveloped basement and both are designed to give children a scientific viewpoint of everyday domestic objects by means of hands-on exhibits. Launch Pad on the first floor is a large, and often crowded, children's area dealing with the practical application of scientific principles to materials, sound, light, heat, energy and electricity through a great number of game-like experiments. You can build things with blocks, move items by rail, weigh bits and pieces on giant scales, feel different metals and even a Van der Graaf generator and generally have lots of fun doing it. Flight Lab on the third floor shows how aircraft fly through a series of hands-on exhibits and there is a simulator where you can experience the thrill of a rollercoaster ride. (There is an additional charge for this but our kids pronounced it well worth the money.) On Air is a mock-up of a radio studio which also contains a computerised mixing-desk where you can create and record your own tunes.

In addition to these galleries, which are specifically aimed at kids, there are also the museum's two newest galleries, Science of Sport and Challenge of Materials. While these two deal with adult topics they do so in a way which undoubtedly appeals to youngsters. The Science of Sport is exactly what the name suggests, a fully interactive gallery examining the influences of science and technology on sport. You can climb a rock face, shoot basketball hoops, test your speed and co-ordination in a number of athletic tests, play golf, tennis and virtual volleyball. There are even simulators which give the feel of driving a bobsleigh or a Formula One racing car or riding a snowboard down a rutted piste. This is a thoroughly enjoyable gallery for all ages and is supervised by a small army of trained assistants who are happy to answer questions or give advice on and help with your sporting endeavours.

The Challenge of Materials seeks to explain the multitude of substances that make up our world: where they come from; what we do with them; what we use them for; and where they go when we have finished with them. This gallery is an absolute revelation and it makes a potentially dull subject extremely interesting and accessible – even for young children. It also contains one of the most amazing objects in the museum – a musical glass bridge spanning the museum's atrium – go there and see it for yourself!
Food for Thought is a partially interactive gallery dealing with how food is produced, packaged, distributed and eaten. The museum does still have quite a number of areas and galleries containing static and glass-enclosed exhibits, some of which are pretty dry and scholarly in terms of both subject and information, but these only seem to heighten the enjoyment of the more innovative galleries.

At peak times there may be a timed ticket system in operation in most popular children's galleries. There is a daily programme of events and a timetable of these is given to you on entry. They range from gallery tours, workshops, films, demonstrations, drama performances or story-telling and can cover any aspects of the museum's contents. There is a museum guidebook at £1.50 and an excellent guidebook for children – the

Explorers Handbook at £3.50; we bought the latter but were so fully occupied by the exhibits that we only opened it once we got home!

HOW TO GET THERE AND WHERE TO PARK
Car: Car-park in Imperial College Road or on-street meter parking.
Underground: South Kensington station has an exit next to the museum entrance.
Train: Victoria station then the underground as above.

OPENING HOURS
All year, daily, 10 a.m.–6 p.m.
Closed: 24–26 December.
Last entry to Science of Sport is at 5 p.m.

ADMISSION
Museum only: Adults: £5.95. Children (5–17), students, unemployed, senior citizens: £3.20. Registered disabled and under-fives: free.
Museum and Science of Sport: Adults: £8.95. Children (5–17), students, unemployed, senior citizens: £5.20. Registered disabled and under-fives: free.
Museum entry free for all visitors after 4.30 p.m. Reduced entry to Science of Sport after 4.30 p.m. Family tickets available.

WHEELCHAIR AND PUSHCHAIR ACCESS
The museums offer more or less full access; there is an Access and Facilities Guide available at the information desk or further information can be obtained by phoning 0171 938 9788.

REFRESHMENTS
The main museum café is located on the ground floor. It's often busy and very crowded with barely room for pushchairs or wheelchairs, although there are several high-chairs. Hot food is served between 12 noon and 3 p.m. with meat dishes from £4.95, vegetarian dishes from £4.75, children's meals at £2.10, sandwiches from £1.80, boxed salads from £2.25, cakes from £1.30, soft drinks 90p, coffee £1.10, tea 90p. You'll find large picnic areas on the first floor and in the basement, next to which are small shops selling drinks and snacks.

SHOP
There is a sports-clothing and footwear shop at the exit from the Science of Sport section and an excellent general shop by the main entrance selling all

manner of fascinating scientific instruments for children as well as postcards, greetings cards, souvenirs, confectionery, games and puzzles. There is also a full-scale Dillons bookshop on site, so there is no shortage of excellent reference and activity books.

TOILET FACILITIES

There is a family room for both mums and dads with baby-changing facilities on the lower-ground, ground, second and third floors.

CLOAKROOM

Available in the basement.

PHOTOGRAPHY

Allowed for personal use only. No tripods or flash allowed.

DOGS

Guide dogs only.

SEGAWORLD

THE TROCADERO, 1 PICCADILLY CIRCUS, LONDON, W1V 8DH
TEL: 0171 734 2777   FAX: 0171 734 7654

HOW LONG SHOULD WE SPEND THERE?
Allow between two to four hours.

WHICH AGE GROUP WILL IT APPEAL TO?
Suitable for all ages (although height restrictions do apply on the 'rides' which will severely reduce younger children's enjoyment).

INTRODUCTION
Most of the attractions we have visited have something to offer for both children and parents; Segaworld, however, is most definitely biased towards the kids although not entirely so if you have a taste for video games. The promotional literature proclaims it to be a 'futuractive theme park' and indeed a theme park it is – albeit an entirely indoor one. As in other theme parks there are rides, seven of them to be precise, but at Segaworld these are, with one exception, virtual-reality rides and so you don't actually go anywhere except in your imagination. This is not to say that they are not exciting, exhilarating even, and the kids in our party got almost as much out of each one as they would have from a white-knuckle roller-coaster. The park is on six levels and is divided into six themed zones and, from the moment you enter on the giant rocket escalator, your senses are assailed by flashing lights and loud pumping rock music which somehow seems to synchronise with the hardware around you. The biggest draws are undoubtedly what Segaworld calls the seven 'ride attractions' which are evenly spread through the building and correspond roughly to each of the zones. The rides are very varied ranging from a flight through space to an underground ride, a deep sea adventure, a futuristic car chase and a ghost hunt; the only non-virtual ride is a kind of 21st-century version

of dodgems with armoured battle carts firing balls at each other in an enclosed arena. The majority of the space in Segaworld is taken up with video games; these can be anything from combat games and ski-racing to motorbike racing and football.

There are so many games that your kids will be spoiled for choice and this is where it can get really expensive. The entrance charge in itself is very low and their Power Pass is an excellent option as it covers entrance and any four of the rides. But, be warned, from then on all ride attractions can very quickly eat up a lot of money. The best approach is to set a financial limit before you start.

There are information points on every level and the staff are, on the whole, pretty helpful (if they can hear you). Each level has numerous change machines dotted around where you can change your notes into the wherewithal for the kids to stick into the games machines and there are also machines where you purchase tickets for the ride attractions. It goes without saying that the Sega brand is relentless but there is so much going on that it is not overly obtrusive. The 'park' is well laid out and easy to get around with escalators and travelators leading from one level to the next but it is a tiring experience for children and adults alike and a little more seating for weary parents would not go amiss! A couple of final things to note are that you have to look neat and tidy or you may be refused entry and that all children under 16 must be accompanied by an adult. Your kids will love Segaworld but it may hurt your ears and pocket!

HOW TO GET THERE AND WHERE TO PARK

Car: On-street parking in the area is very limited but there are a number of car-parks within a short walking distance, the nearest ones being in Brewer Street or Whitcomb Street (be prepared for very high central London parking charges).

Underground: Piccadilly Circus station (Piccadilly and Bakerloo lines) has an exit directly into The Trocadero Centre itself – just follow the signs. Leicester Square station (Piccadilly and Northern lines) is a five-minute walk away.

OPENING HOURS

All year, daily, 10 a.m.–12 a.m. (last entrance is at 10.30 p.m.).
Closed: 25 December.
They do occasionally have private functions so it may be best to call in advance.

ADMISSION

Adults and children: £2. Children under 1.10 metres tall and disabled: free. All ride attractions and video games are paid for as taken. The ride attractions are either £2 or £3 per person and the video games are either 50p or £1 a go. A Power Pass (includes entrance and any four ride attractions) costs £7.90 per person.

WHEELCHAIR AND PUSHCHAIR ACCESS

There is full wheelchair access to all areas of the site. Although entrance to Segaworld is by a giant escalator, there is a lift from ground level to the top-level entrance (at the time of writing this was being replaced so it may be best to check in advance to make sure that this has been completed). Once inside there is plenty of space to manoeuvre both wheelchairs and pushchairs on every level; moving from one level to another is either by travelator which presents no problems for wheels or by escalator which may be a little more tricky and obviously requires the help of either an assistant or a carer in the case of wheelchairs. There are a number of special wheelchair lifts around the site where places are accessed by steps. All the ride attractions can be accessed by disabled visitors with assistance.

REFRESHMENTS

The options on site are really not that exciting. There are McDonald's on levels three and one selling the usual reasonably priced fast food and levels four and two have Sega's own SplishSplashSplosh refreshment centres selling a limited range of snacks, soft drinks and sweets. You are not allowed to bring your own food or drink into Segaworld. If you don't want to take advantage of Segaworld's catering there are, of course, a myriad of choices to suit every taste and budget within a few minutes' walk as this is central London.

SHOP

The Segastore is located just outside the exit on level one and sells a wide range of gifts, clothing and console games. Everything is Sega branded and related as you might expect. Precious little in the way of pocket-money toys though.

TOILET FACILITIES

There are toilets on all levels with specific family and disabled toilets plus baby-changing facilities provided on levels six and four.

CLOAKROOM
There is a cloakroom available.

PHOTOGRAPHY
Allowed throughout and there is even a themed photo area on level four.

DOGS
Guide dogs only.

THE TATE GALLERY

MILLBANK, LONDON, SW1P 4RG
TEL: 0171 887 8008 (RECORDED INFORMATION) / 0171 887 8000

HOW LONG SHOULD WE SPEND THERE?
Allow two hours.

WHICH AGE GROUP WILL IT APPEAL TO?
On the whole not suitable for under-fives except for the Sunday activity trolley.

INTRODUCTION
This is a rather grown-up experience as the Tate houses the national collections of British art and modern art from around the world. Despite some of it being rather impenetrable, the gallery is nonetheless worth a visit either to tie in with a school project or on a Sunday when there is a children's activity trolley. Although this may not sound terribly exciting the children really enjoyed it; they are issued with a wallet and tray containing glue, scissors, paper, crayons and gummed paper and an activity sheet and are set to work. The gallery was full of budding artists making the most of the material and it seemed to be really quite successful judging by the pride with which each work was submitted for inspection. The trolley is located in a different gallery each Sunday so ask at the reception and also pick up the children's trail brochure. This brochure is a little disappointing and could be made far more imaginative, but it still helps to make the visit more
worth while. Alternatively pick up an activity book in the bookshop (£2.50) before you start. This is pitched at older children and nicely prepared. You can't hope to get around the entire gallery without a lot of whingeing from younger members of the family so content yourselves with short bursts. Call for details of holiday activities and free tours.

161

HOW TO GET THERE AND WHERE TO PARK

Car: Car-park in John Islip Street behind the gallery or meter-parking in surrounding streets.

Underground: A five-minute walk from Pimlico station.

Train: A 30-minute walk from Victoria station.

OPENING HOURS

All year, daily, 10 a.m.–5 p.m.

Closed: 24–26 December.

ADMISSION

Free, but donations are welcomed.

WHEELCHAIR AND PUSHCHAIR ACCESS

Enter through the Clore Gallery to avoid the steps at the main entrance. From there you can take a lift and after that it's easy. There's also a lift in the Friends' Gallery to the lower floor where the Tate café and restaurant are located. Wheelchairs are available.

REFRESHMENTS

The Tate café is open between 10.30 a.m. and 5.30 p.m. with good-quality food on offer. Unusual drinks such as elderflower pressé are included amongst the more normal selection. Funghi trifolati at £4.95, scones for £1.35, flapjacks at £1.20, vegetarian quiche for £3, sandwiches from £1.95 with standard fillings as well as for more exotic tastes, such as blue brie and loganberry. Home-made soup and roll £2.50. The café was very crowded when we visited and it was difficult to find a table. We spotted six high-chairs. Eat your picnic in the gallery gardens or by the river.

SHOP

The shop is open from Monday to Saturday, 10.30 a.m. to 5.40 p.m. and Sunday from 10 a.m. to 5.40 p.m. A very adult affair with lots of beautiful greetings cards, postcards and posters featuring Tate Gallery exhibits and a huge array of books. There is also a small book corner for children.

TOILET FACILITIES

Baby-changing facilities are found in the ladies' toilet on the ground floor of the Clore Gallery. Wheelchair access is possible in these toilets and in those next to the main entrance.

CLOAKROOM
Supervised cloakroom.

PHOTOGRAPHY
Not allowed in special exhibitions but permitted in the other galleries as long as it's for private use.

DOGS
Not allowed.

THORPE PARK

STAINES ROAD, CHERTSEY, SURREY
TEL: 01932 562633 (RECORDED INFORMATION)/0990 880 880

HOW LONG SHOULD WE SPEND THERE?
Allow all day.

WHICH AGE GROUP WILL IT APPEAL TO?
Suitable for all ages.

INTRODUCTION
To an adult Thorpe Park has the kind of faded glamour of an ageing fairground, as if it was grand once and is struggling to keep pace with modern technology. The children, of course, see nothing of this and thoroughly enjoy the attractions. There is more for younger children than for older ones – we found ourselves doing several repeat visits to the more adventurous rides for our nine-year-old while there seemed to be more scope for our six-year-old. We visited on a sunny late-October weekend and the queues were negligible, but we have also been in high summer and endured long waits for the popular rides. The older visitor will enjoy Thunder River. While you don't get a drenching there's still excitement at the odd splash. The Flying Fish ride is surprisingly fierce and not for the faint-hearted although we did see some quite young unaccompanied children on this. Nearby the Tea-cup ride is a firm favourite – you should choose one of the cups on the revolving sections of the platform if you want a wilder ride. The Wicked Witches Haunt is hugely disappointing if you've experienced other more imaginative and scarier rides, but the Loggers Leap – although short – is thrilling. If you want to see what excited terror looks like then examine the automatic photographs as you leave the ride; they'll set you back around £4 to buy but just looking at them on the screens will raise a smile. The other two rides which could be described as

thrilling are Depth Charge (long waits for a five-second ride down a wet bumpy slide in a boat) and the newly constructed X:\No Way Out which, by all accounts, is fairly scary. After a long walk inside, a backwards ride in pitch darkness awaits as you are taken on a rough, fast roller-coaster journey with frequent abrupt stops and disorientating sound effects. There's a height restriction of 1.4m but smaller ones can be entertained in the Octopuses Garden while you wait. The Calgary Stampede is another recommended ride.

Gentle pursuits include taking either the waterbus to Thorpe Farm, which was built in the 1930s, a train ride around the park and the Viking Rowers – a leisurely row around an enclosed area of the park lake. Height restrictions apply on many of the rides; 0.9–1.2 metres is the lowest but this often means simply having to be accompanied by an adult.

HOW TO GET THERE AND WHERE TO PARK

Car: Take junction 11 or 13 off the M25 and simply follow the signs. (*Don't take junction 12 as, although the park is right next to it, this junction only accesses the M3.*) The main entrance is signposted off the A320. If approaching from another direction the park is clearly signposted throughout the area.

Train: From Waterloo to Staines station then either a ten-minute taxi ride or a 30-minute walk to the park.

OPENING HOURS

Variable opening and closing dates each year but essentially early February to early November, 9.30 a.m. to 7.30 p.m. in high season and 10 a.m. to 5 p.m. in low season.

ADMISSION

Adults: £16.50. Children (under-14): £13. Under one metre: free. *Disabled visitors*: Adults: £13. Children (under-14): £10. Family ticket: £12.50 per person for any combination of four or more visitors – only available if booked by 5.30 p.m. at least one day in advance.

All rides are included in the entrance price.

WHEELCHAIR AND PUSHCHAIR ACCESS

While the park itself is smooth and flat, many rides are accessed up steps so pushchairs may have to be abandoned. They claim that all rides except Depth Charge and X:\No Way Out are accessible to wheelchair users. Wheelchair loan and free special wheelchair guide available. Call 0990 880 880 for further details.

REFRESHMENTS
Expect lowest common denominator catering and lots of it; Burger King, KFC, fish and chips and other varieties of fast food. Plenty of benches and an undercover area for picnics.

SHOP
Plenty of shops dotted around selling every type of cheap tat imaginable!

TOILET FACILITIES
Baby-changing available on the upper level of the Dome, at Thorpe Farm, Canada Creek and Central Park. The nursing mothers' facility is situated in Central Park and Canada Creek. Wheelchair-access toilets are available.

CLOAKROOM
Coin-operated storage beneath the Dome by the Depth Charge.

PHOTOGRAPHY
Allowed and film sold.

DOGS
Guide dogs only.

TOWER OF LONDON

TOWER HILL, LONDON, EC3
TEL: 0171 709 0765

HOW LONG SHOULD WE SPEND THERE?
Allow two hours.

WHICH AGE GROUP WILL IT APPEAL TO?
Suitable for all ages.

INTRODUCTION
The Tower is slightly disappointing; as one of the two or three high-profile attractions in the country it promises rather more than it delivers. You almost get the feeling that you are expected to be reverential with regard to its history which is, of course, impressive, but it does little to truly inform or bring alive the experience, particularly for children. With all the technological innovations utilised in other attractions, none seem to have been deployed here – perhaps it was felt that it would not be in keeping – but having seen how the sympathetic use of video, audio and hands-on displays can really enhance an experience it seems a pity that this hasn't been done here, particularly given the price. Instead of watching endless old newsreel footage of the Queen's coronation while queuing to see the Crown Jewels, it would have been so much more interesting to hear more about the history of the Tower itself – even more detailed signs would have been an improvement. But then it still continues to attract a colossal number of visitors year after year.

It would be difficult not to be impressed with the Crown Jewels – despite the speed with which you are rushed past them on a moving walkway! No doubt this is a necessary addition given the length of the

167

queues to get into the Jewel House. Regrettably two of the attractions guaranteed to appeal to young imaginations, the instruments of torture and the armoury, have been moved from the Tower and the brief description put on show around the Tower of the ravens pecking out the eyes of beheaded victims didn't make up for this. The site is particularly worthwhile if the children are studying the Tudors at school and seeing the spot where Anne Boleyn (amongst others) was beheaded is a vivid history lesson.

One way in which you can get more out of the visit is to join one of the frequent tours conducted by the famous Yeoman warders who really do talk with enthusiasm and animation and who divulge all those little bits of information which help to make the visit more memorable. The groups do get very large, however, and it can be difficult to hear. Special events and guidebook cost £3.50.

HOW TO GET THERE AND WHERE TO PARK
Car: Car-park in the Minories, which is a ten-minute walk away, and costs just £2 for a full day on Saturdays, Sundays and bank holidays.
Underground: A five-minute walk from Tower Hill station.
Train: From Fenchurch Street station or Docklands Light Railway to Tower Gateway.
Boat: Take a short boat ride down the Thames to Tower pier from Charing Cross pier.

OPENING HOURS
Summer, Monday to Saturday, 9 a.m.–5.30 p.m. Sunday, 10 a.m.–5.30 p.m.
Winter, Monday to Saturday, 9 a.m.–4.30 p.m. Sunday, 10 a.m.–4.30 p.m.
Closed: 1 January, 24–26 December.

ADMISSION
Adults: £6.95. Children (4–15), senior citizens and students: £4.95. Family ticket (two adults and two children): £15.95.

WHEELCHAIR AND PUSHCHAIR ACCESS
Very restricted although the access through the Jewel House is fine.

REFRESHMENTS
There are no cafés on site, however, there is a simple refreshment barrow at the Tower serving coffee, muffins and cold drinks but the nearest eaterie is a Prêt a Manger café on the wharf outside the Tower which serves a

selection of freshly made sandwiches, cakes, hot and cold drinks. The other alternative is McDonald's and other similar restaurants in the complex near the bookshop. The best place for a picnic is on one of the many benches along the riverside walk.

SHOP
There is relentless merchandising in the Tower! The West Gate shop is a large but very good gift shop opposite the main entrance to the Tower offering a small range of royal and historical books for kids, confectionery, toiletries and postcards. It gets terribly crowded and there is much of the same range at the many shops inside the Tower.

TOILET FACILITIES
Baby-changing facilities and wheelchair-access toilets are found behind the Jewel House.

CLOAKROOM
No.

PHOTOGRAPHY
Not allowed in the Jewel House.

DOGS
Guide dogs only.

VERULAMIUM MUSEUM

ST MICHAEL'S, ST ALBANS, HERTFORDSHIRE
TEL: 01727 819339   FAX: 01727 859919

HOW LONG SHOULD WE SPEND THERE?
Allow one to two hours.

WHICH AGE GROUP WILL IT APPEAL TO?
Suitable for over-fours.

INTRODUCTION
An excellent small, but award-winning museum situated on the site of the
Roman city of Verulamium that aims to depict everyday life in the city from
its founding to its ruin.

The museum is spacious with clear pictorial and text boards which take
you through various displays from the Iron Age to the present day. There
are numerous artefacts excavated from the site: beautifully restored
mosaics, recreated Roman rooms and a fascinating room dedicated to
Roman burials with an award-winning display accompanied by an
attention-grabbing video. A roving curator will answer your questions and
a couple of touch-screen databases give extra details about particular
exhibits in a child-friendly way. You can examine Roman coins through a
microscope, build a Roman arch and watch X-rays of Roman pots. We
picked up some simple quiz sheets at the entrance for 10p (there were three
levels of difficulty) and these were an effective way of getting the children
to focus on the exhibits.

The museum is undoubtedly the main attraction but there are
remnants of the actual city walls and the hypocaust – the underground
heating system – in the large municipal park behind the museum that

covers much of the site of the old Verulamium and if the children want to get rid of some energy you could do far worse than let them feed the ducks, explore the equipment in the play area or play crazy golf. A football and wellies may be useful accessories. The Roman theatre can be reached across the main road beyond the museum and has separate limited parking.

HOW TO GET THERE AND WHERE TO PARK

Car: Exit junction 6 off M1 on to the A405 then take the B4630 and follow the brown signs. Also exit junction 9 or 7 off the M1 or junction 21A off the M25 then follow the directions above. Pay-and-display car-park adjacent to the site is very reasonable at just 30p for all day but it was surprisingly busy the Sunday afternoon we visited.

Train: To St Albans City station by Thameslink from King's Cross or St Albans Abbey station from Euston or Watford Junction. You can then catch the 300 bus to St Michael's village disembarking at the request stop at the school – the museum is opposite the school.

OPENING HOURS

March to October, Monday to Saturday, 10 a.m.–5.30 p.m. Sunday, 2 p.m.–5 p.m.
November to February, Monday to Saturday, 10 a.m.–4 p.m. Sunday, 2 p.m.–4 p.m.
Closed: 25 December.

ADMISSION

Adults: £2.80. Children (over five), senior citizens, and concessions: £1.60. Family ticket (two adults and two children): £7. Under-fives: free.

WHEELCHAIR AND PUSHCHAIR ACCESS

Access is very good around the museum and the spacious park can be negotiated on tarmac paths and with slightly more difficulty on the grass.

REFRESHMENTS

None on site but there is a café in the park. This is a five-minute walk from the museum and is on the flat so it can be easily reached by both wheelchairs and pushchairs. It serves very reasonably priced coffee at 65p, tea at 30p and even cappuccino at 85p. Squash and fizzy drinks were also available at 24–40p and sandwiches were £1.50. They also have ice-cream and sweets – nothing inspired but adequate for a quick snack. Two high-chairs were visible, and four tables and benches outside supplemented the

171

indoor seating. Opening hours can be erratic and if you are willing to go as far as the street in front of the museum there is a pub called The Six Bells that serves home-made food all week and states that families are welcome. There is also the coffee shop at the Mill Museum just a little further down the same street and adjacent to this, the Egon Ronay-recommended Waffle House; we would have tried this but the queues to get in were too long! We can only deduce that the waffles are worth the wait.

SHOP
The shop is located around the exit and entrance area and sells a limited range of topical books, replicas, souvenirs, pocket-money toys and a guide to Verulamium at £3. An unexpected discovery was the Herts and Middlesex Wildlife Trust shop just beyond the park gates. The shop is small but tastefully stocked with wildlife-themed cards, pottery, games and walking books and has a small room for children with imaginative but unsophisticated exhibits, including wooden puzzles for the smaller children and quiz sheets about information in the room.

TOILET FACILITIES
None on site. Public toilets inconveniently placed in the adjacent car-park have wheelchair access. There is no special parent-and-baby room but the ladies' toilet had a changing table. There didn't appear to be any specific closure times for the toilet despite their public location.

CLOAKROOM
No supervised room but there are rails in the exit corridor where things can be left at your own risk.

PHOTOGRAPHY
Allowed and film sold at reception.

DOGS
Guide dogs only allowed inside the museum. All dogs allowed in the park.

WATERHALL FARM AND CRAFT CENTRE

WHITWELL, HITCHIN, HERTS, SG4 8BN
TEL: 01 438 871 256

HOW LONG SHOULD WE SPEND THERE?
Allow two hours.

WHICH AGE GROUP WILL IT APPEAL TO?
Suitable for all ages.

INTRODUCTION
Of the many farms we have visited in Hertfordshire, this is by no means the most sophisticated but it delighted the children with its hands-on approach. They could actually climb inside some of the pens and play with the tame animals which included rabbits, guinea pigs, calves, goats and piglets. There are horses and donkeys too, and rare breeds of sheep, pigs, as well as many hens and ducks that can be seen on the brief circular walk through the farm's paddocks. A short miniature railway ride across the paddock costs 50p and leaves twice a day. An additional attraction is a small cluster of craft shops around the café. These include a carpentry shop with workshop on the premises, as well as shops selling wrought-iron work, plants and antique pine furniture; it all seemed reasonably priced and afforded a more adult distraction while the children made use of the sandpit and hay-bale room.

HOW TO GET THERE AND WHERE TO PARK
Car: Exit the A1(M) for the B656 to Hitchin, at Codicote follow signs for

Whitwell with the entrance off the B651 Whitwell–Hitchin road. Limited space in the car-park so it could be very crowded in summer.
Train: You could get a train to Stevenage from King's Cross but you would have to make your own way to the farm by bus or taxi.

OPENING HOURS
All year, Wednesday to Sunday, 10 a.m.–5 p.m.
Closed: Monday and Tuesday (except on bank holidays and during the school holidays); 25–26 December.

ADMISSION
Adults: £2.75. Children (2–16) and senior citizens: £1.50. Under-twos: free.

WHEELCHAIR AND PUSHCHAIR ACCESS
Access is possible around the farmyard and buildings and the café area but the circular walk is only just negotiable with a pushchair and not recommended with a wheelchair.

REFRESHMENTS
A small café with outdoor seating in the yard and opening hours as the farm itself. Food was good with cream teas (£2.50), toasted tea-cakes, flapjacks, shortbread, toasted and regular sandwiches and ploughman's on offer. There are no high-chairs and it's a tight squeeze for pushchairs inside. Own food is accepted outside if the tables aren't all being used by customers but you may feel more comfortable picnicking in one of the fields.

SHOP
Packed with many items; very animal themed but some quite tasteful things amongst the more usual offerings and the goods are not expensive.

TOILET FACILITIES
Located near the café with disabled access. Very basic baby-changing facilities in ladies' toilets in a rather draughty Portakabin.

CLOAKROOM
No cloakroom as such but the friendly staff will be happy to help out if you need to store anything during your visit.

PHOTOGRAPHY
Allowed and the shop sells film but it is not always in stock so it is safer to bring your own.

DOGS
Only guide dogs admitted around the farm buildings but there is a separate circular walk which dogs are allowed on through the paddocks.

WESTMINSTER ABBEY

BROAD SANCTUARY, LONDON, SW1
TEL: 0171 222 5152

HOW LONG SHOULD WE SPEND THERE?
Allow about one hour.

WHICH AGE GROUP WILL IT APPEAL TO?
Suitable for all ages.

INTRODUCTION
This is one of the most splendid and beautiful historical buildings in Britain, and if you are fortunate enough to visit during a service you'll be hard pushed not to be moved by the wonderful sound of the Westminster Boys' Choir – although a large part of the main cathedral is inaccessible during services. The best part for children is the brass rubbing in the cloisters (from £2.50 depending on the size of the brass rubbing). You'll find the Abbey particularly stimulating for children's history lessons; nine English kings and queens are buried in St Edward's Chapel and Elizabeth I's remains can be found in Henry VII's Chapel. The Coronation Chair is to be removed from the shrine of St Edward the Confessor and placed on a plinth in the cathedral for permanent viewing. In the museum you'll find the second Coronation Chair used by William and Mary, the rehearsal coronation jewels, wax effigies made from the death masks of various kings and queens and archaeological finds from the Abbey site.

Also part of the museum is the Pyx Chamber which was used as a royal treasury for over 400 years and is now used to display some of the Abbey's treasures. Another interesting feature is the College Garden which occupies an area that has been under continuous cultivation for over 900 years since its origin as the Abbey's infirmary garden. It would once have been a source of food and medicine for the monks, with fruit trees, vegetables and a variety of medicinal herbs being cultivated. It would also have been a place of tranquil relaxation and gentle exercise, a function which it fulfils today for the Abbey staff and the public. The garden is open on Tuesdays and Thursdays throughout the year.

HOW TO GET THERE AND WHERE TO PARK

Car: Car-park on Great College Street opposite the Houses of Parliament. There are meters in the surrounding streets but these are very expensive.

Underground: Opposite Westminster station or a ten-minute walk from St James's Park station.

Train: Victoria station then the underground to one of the above stations.

OPENING HOURS

Cathedral: All year, Monday to Friday, 9.30 a.m.–4 p.m. Saturday, 9.30 a.m.–2 p.m. and 3.45 p.m.–5 p.m. Sundays, open for services only.
Museum: Opening hours as above.

ADMISSION

From 1998 access to the Abbey will change and will be via the North door where an entrance fee will be payable.
Adults: £5. Senior citizens: £3. Children (5–15): £2.

WHEELCHAIR AND PUSHCHAIR ACCESS

Pushchair access is through the main entrance only and wheelchair access is through the Dean's Yard and cloister and through the Poets' Corner exit. Ring the doorbell to call the doorman who will be able to assist you. Henry VII's Chapel is not accessible to wheelchairs.

REFRESHMENTS

The Abbey coffee shop is located in the cloisters; a small restaurant area where you can buy exotically flavoured coffees for a pound, tea at 95p, hot chocolate at £1.40 and soft drinks for a pound. There is not a wide selection of food but they do sell fresh sandwiches at £1.90 or £2.95 and muffins. The limited selection is somewhat compensated by the remarkable surroundings – there's something rather special about sitting on the ancient stone cloister benches with the beautiful courtyards as background. There is also a kiosk outside the Abbey. While you cannot bring your own food into the Abbey environs you may like to take a picnic down to the riverbank which is just a short walk away.

SHOP
Small shop and bookshop by the main entrance.

TOILET FACILITIES
None on site but public toilets across the road next to the Queen Elizabeth Conference Centre with wheelchair access but no baby-changing facilities.

CLOAKROOM
No.
PHOTOGRAPHY
Not allowed.

DOGS
Guide dogs only.

WHIPSNADE TREE CATHEDRAL

THE GREEN, WHIPSNADE, BEDFORDSHIRE
TEL: 01494 528051 (NATIONAL TRUST)

HOW LONG SHOULD WE SPEND THERE?
Allow one hour.

WHICH AGE GROUP WILL IT APPEAL TO?
Suitable for all ages.

INTRODUCTION
The Tree Cathedral, now managed by the National Trust, is an unusual venue and its success depends largely on how much your children enjoy the outdoors. Unless you're very lucky they will almost certainly not appreciate the feat of imagination that led to its creation but they'll enjoy a picnic by the dew pond and the wonderful walk along the Dunstable Downs. The Tree Cathedral was created between 1931 and 1938 and consists of many species of tree which were carefully planted to the traditional pattern of a cathedral to commemorate three of the friends of a Mr Blyth, two of whom died during World War I. Spiritual in origin, it still conveys a wonderful sense of tranquillity, even to the most irreligious visitor, while allowing the children to run around and noisily play hide-and-seek in the 'nave' and 'transept'. You can easily gain access from the back of the cathedral to walks along the Dunstable Downs, an escarpment affording marvellous views and on a fine day you can admire the gliders drifting high above the tiny airfield. A conveniently placed, if busy, car-park should have a welcome ice-cream van if you make it this far (about two and a half miles) and we were lucky enough to witness the antics of a stunt kite-flying team.

179

HOW TO GET THERE AND WHERE TO PARK

Car: Exit M1 by junction 9 and follow the A5 to Dunstable then the B4540 to Whipsnade Park Zoo. As you cross the junction with the B541 you approach a pub on the left, opposite which is a track next to a tiny green which leads to the Tree Cathedral. Limited free parking by the entrance.

OPENING HOURS

All daylight hours. There is an annual service held at the end of June.

ADMISSION

Free.

WHEELCHAIR AND PUSHCHAIR ACCESS

Manageable in the cathedral but not on the walks.

REFRESHMENTS

None on site but there is a pub on the main road which serves food (although we haven't tried this) and, with luck, on a fine day there should be an ice-cream van in the car-park on Dunstable Downs.

SHOP

No.

TOILET FACILITIES

No.

CLOAKROOM

No.

PHOTOGRAPHY

Allowed.

DOGS

Allowed.

WHIPSNADE WILD ANIMAL PARK

DUNSTABLE, BEDFORDSHIRE, LU6 2LF
TEL: 01582 872171/01582 872649

HOW LONG SHOULD WE SPEND THERE?
Allow four to five hours.

WHICH AGE GROUP WILL IT APPEAL TO?
Suitable for all ages.

INTRODUCTION
Whipsnade is a fairly expensive option for a day out, but it does offer good value for money – especially if you steer clear of the poor catering and take your own food. Naturally there's a splendid range of wild animals: elephants, chimpanzees, dignified white and black rhino, mud-bound hippos, indifferent Siberian tigers, wolves, brown bears and many, many more. While the animals are not quite in their natural habitats they did have considerably more room than just a concrete compound to move around in. The bears' area is wonderfully overgrown, making glimpses of the animals all the more rewarding. There's also a children's farm, bird garden (with tiny baby penguins freshly incubated) and a Discovery Centre (open from 10.30 a.m. to 30 minutes before the park closes); the latter is an indoor feature with displays of snakes, spiders, ants, crocodiles and all the creatures that children both fear and are inescapably drawn to.

There is a programme of talks and displays (detailed on the timetable given to you on entry) throughout the day – we only made it to the flying display in the Arena when we saw the macaws flying in formation and magnificent hawks swooping low over our heads to catch prey in mid-air. If the walk around the park is daunting you can take your car round (paying extra for the privilege) or pick up the free open-top bus which will drop you at conveniently placed stops. An added extra is the Whipsnade railway which tours the park, tickets are priced at £1.80 for adults and 90p for children and the train leaves every hour from 1 p.m. – weather permitting.

HOW TO GET THERE AND WHERE TO PARK

Car: Exit junction 9 of M1 and follow A5 towards Dunstable, then follow the brown tourist signs to the park. Large free car-park opposite the main entrance.

OPENING HOURS

All year, daily, 10 a.m.–7 p.m. (last admission 6 p.m.).

ADMISSION

Adults: £8.50. Children (3–15), students and senior citizens: £7. No family ticket. Under-threes: free. Cars taken into the park: £6.50.

WHEELCHAIR AND PUSHCHAIR ACCESS

Excellent wheelchair and pushchair access throughout the park with easily negotiable tarmac paths everywhere.

REFRESHMENTS

There are picnic benches dotted everywhere which on balance are a better option than the catering facilities which are very average. The Look Out café has a pleasant position with picture windows looking out over Dunstable Downs. Burger, fries and side salad at £3.95 was typical of the hot food on offer with a thoroughly unimaginative and poor-quality children's menu of burger and chips or sausage and chips at £2.95. There were also sandwiches, synthetic-looking Danish pastries, tea at 55p, coffee at 80p, squash at 45p and canned drinks at 70p. There were no high-chairs but there was plenty of space for buggies. There is also a proper restaurant called The Cafe on the Lake but nothing compares with the magnificent picnic sites outside the Look Out café or by the lion enclosure where there are benches but no tables with both having fantastic views.

SHOP

Chaotic and rather tacky. Great if you need a fridge magnet or a keyring. Unsurprisingly almost totally animal-related merchandise.

TOILET FACILITIES

There are toilets by the main gate, on the way to the Look Out café and by the Café on the Lake. All have wheelchair access and baby-changing facilities – albeit rather basic.

CLOAKROOM

No.

PHOTOGRAPHY

Allowed and film is sold in the shop.

DOGS

Guide dogs only.

WIMPOLE PARK AND GARDENS AND HOME FARM

ARRINGTON, NR ROYSTON, CAMBRIDGESHIRE, SG8 0BW
TEL: 01223 207257/01223 207001 (EVENTS BOOKING)/
01223 208670 (THE OLD RECTORY RESTAURANT)

HOW LONG SHOULD WE SPEND THERE?
Allow all day but it can be split up as follows: house, one hour; farm, one and a half hours; gardens and estate, endless.

WHICH AGE GROUP WILL IT APPEAL TO?
Suitable for all ages.

INTRODUCTION
Situated in beautiful countryside, this enormous park offers a whole day's activities. If you also enjoy making the most of the many marked trails then buy a map, costing £1, which will show you the routes. Alternatively you can wander at will among the formal aspects of the estate, such as the gardens and the avenue leading to the folly and to the remnants of the late-17th-century landscaping fashions or you can opt to take the more natural woodland walks – any of which can take an hour or much more.

The hall, first built in 1640, can be made more interesting for young visitors by purchasing the children's guidebook which, at £1.25, offers excellent value. Each room is described in simple terms with snippets of information that would excite a child's imagination and sets tasks which focus darting minds on the room itself such as 'spot the hidden door'. The hall is beautifully preserved and its rooms filled with furniture and

184

artefacts of the times, including a library with over 7,000 leather-bound books and a pretty collection of period matchboxes. Inevitably it is the more mundane aspects of life in the late 1700s which are fascinating – such as the room-size plunge bath and the wooden shower complete with hand-driven pump – but nothing more so than the below-stairs rooms such as the dry store with its tea-chests on runners and the named bells for calling servants upstairs. A full colour guidebook is also available for £4.50 and more modest leaflets costing from 60p each are also available. You can choose to take the periodic shirehorse-drawn cart from the table block to the farm for 70p each way (by showing farm entrance tickets first), or walk through the formal gardens which will take around ten minutes. The working farm with its beautiful black wooden thatched barns is great fun. Pick up a bag of animal feed at the entrance for 20p and stroll among the pens of goats, kids, cows, calves, pigs and horses. Trip over a bewildering array of breeds of hen and step into the lamb paddock – make sure that toddlers are closely supervised as some of the larger lambs were quite boisterous and not averse to jumping up if they smell the animal feed. There were various activities going on the weekend we visited, such as mucking out the pigs, milking the goats and sheep-shearing at various times of the day.

There's an enclosed toddlers' play area with ride-on toy tractors, a sandpit and a 'house' and play equipment for older children too. Home crafts are often demonstrated in one of the barns and there's a display of old carts and farm implements in another.

Make your way back to the stable block (by cart if you prefer) where there's a second-hand bookshop and yet more carts on display. Pick up an events leaflet at the ticket office.

HOW TO GET THERE AND WHERE TO PARK

Car: Located eight miles south-west of Cambridge on the A603. Signposted off M11 at junction 12. Large, free car-park. Disabled car-parking near the entrance.

Train: About an hour's journey from King's Cross to Royston station. It is then about a seven-mile taxi ride to the hall.

OPENING HOURS

Park: All year, daily, dawn–dusk (except 18–20 July, dawn–5.30 p.m.).
Hall: 22 March to 1 August and 1 September to 2 November, Tuesday to Thursday and the weekends, 1 p.m.–5 p.m. August, Tuesday to Sunday, 1 p.m.–5 p.m. Also open on bank holiday Mondays, 11 a.m.–5 p.m.
Farm: 8 March to 2 November, daily (except Monday and Friday). Also

open on bank holiday Mondays. Open seven days a week during July and August, 10.30 a.m.–5 p.m. Winter, open Wednesday, Saturday and Sunday, 11 a.m.–4 p.m.

ADMISSION
Hall and Farm: Adults: £7. Children (3–16): £3.50.
Hall only: Adults: £5.20. Children (3–16): £2.25.
Farm only: Adults: £4. Children (3–16): £2.50.
Wheelchair users pay full price but carers are admitted free. Under-threes: free.

WHEELCHAIR AND PUSHCHAIR ACCESS
Access for the gardens and the farm is fine, but it is very limited in the hall. Even if you can negotiate the steps at the main entrance, pushchairs are not welcome at all (baby-slings are available) and there is no wheelchair access to the basement or second floor. Wheelchairs are available on loan at the ticket office.

REFRESHMENTS
There is a small café at the farm serving hot drinks, cold drinks, a few cakes and sandwiches from £1.75, soup and a roll £1.75 and ice-cream and crisps are also available. Nothing to particularly recommend the food but there is a spacious room with four high-chairs and a well-equipped indoor play area. There are also benches and tables outside that can be used for your own picnic. A similar arrangement is found at the stable block, although smaller, and I'm not sure that own food will be quite so welcomed at the outside tables. Still there's masses of open space on the estate for picnics but no shelter if you get a downpour. The Old Rectory Restaurant is a more recent addition, serving full meals in a more formal setting.

SHOP
The shop at the farm has a small selection of National Trust merchandise but a broader range can be found at the main shop in the stable block – from wine and sweaters to quality pocket-money toys, books and puzzles.

TOILET FACILITIES
A baby-changing room and separate wheelchair-access toilet are to be found in the stable block and at the farm. I noticed a thoughtfully placed child's step in the farm toilet. Wheelchair-access toilet only in the hall and bear in mind that the stable block is a fair walk from the hall and a long walk from the farm.

CLOAKROOM
No.

PHOTOGRAPHY
Not allowed inside the hall but fine elsewhere.

DOGS
Guide dogs only in the hall, farm and gardens. Dogs welcome in the park if kept under control as there are sheep.

VENUES AT A GLANCE

Attraction	Region	Weather	Car Parking	Tube	Train	Opening Season	Disabled Access	Dogs Allowed?	Restaurant
Arundel Castle	South	Both	Yes	No	Yes	Part	Full	Guide	Yes
Bekonscot Model Village	North	Fair	Yes	No	Yes	Part	Full	Guide	Yes
HMS *Belfast*	Central	Both	No	Yes	Yes	All	Part	Guide	Yes
Bethnal Green Museum of Childhood	East	Wet	Yes	Yes	Yes	All	Part	Guide	Yes
Bluebell Railway	South	Both	Yes	No	Yes	All	Part	Guide	Yes
Boat Trip on the Thames	Central/East	Both	No	Yes	No	All	Full	Yes	No
Britain At War Experience	Central/South	Wet	No	Yes	Yes	All	Full	Guide	No
British Museum	Central	Wet	No	Yes	No	All	Full	Guide	Yes
Buckinghamshire Railway Centre	North	Fair	Yes	No	Yes	Part	Part	Yes	Yes
Cabinet War Rooms	Central	Wet	No	Yes	No	All	Full	Guide	No
Chiltern Open-Air Museum	West	Fair	Yes	No	No	Part	Part	Yes	Yes
Design Museum	Central/South	Wet	No	Yes	Yes	All	Full	Guide	Yes

Attraction	Region	Weather							
Didcot Railway Centre	West	Fair	Yes	No	Yes	Part	Part	Yes	Yes
Duxford Airfield	North	Both	Yes	No	No	Part	Full	Guide	Yes
Epping Forest	East	Fair	Yes	Yes	Yes	All	Part	Yes	No
Geffrye Museum	East	Wet	No	Yes	Yes	All	Full	Guide	Yes
Globe Theatre	Central/South	Wet	No	Yes	Yes	All	Full	Guide	Yes
Hampton Court Palace	South	Both	Yes	No	Yes	All	Part	Guide	Yes
Hatfield House & Gardens	North	Both	Yes	No	Yes	Part	Full	Yes	Yes
Holland Park	Central	Fair	Yes	Yes	No	All	Full	Yes	Yes
House on the Hill Toy Museum	North	Wet	Yes	No	Yes	Part	Part	Guide	No
Imperial War Museum	Central/South	Wet	No	Yes	Yes	All	Full	Guide	Yes
Kew Bridge Steam Museum	Central/South	Wet	Yes	Yes	No	All	Part	Guide	Yes
Knebworth House & Park	North	Both	Yes	No	No	Part	Part	Yes	Yes
Leeds Castle	South	Both	Yes	No	Yes	All	Full	Guide	Yes
Legoland Windsor	West	Fair	Yes	No	No	Part	Full	Guide	Yes
Little Venice Canal Trip	Central/North	Both	No	Yes	No	Yes	Part	Guide	No

Attraction	Region	Weather	Car Parking	Tube	Train	Opening Season	Disabled Access	Dogs Allowed?	Restaurant
London Aquarium	Central	Wet	No	Yes	No	Yes	Full	Guide	Yes
London Canal Museum	Central/North	Wet	No	Yes	Yes	All	Part	Guide	No
London Dungeon	Central/South	Wet	No	Yes	Yes	All	Full	Guide	Yes
London Toy And Model Museum	Central	Wet	Yes	Yes	Yes	All	Part	Guide	Yes
London Transport Museum	Central	Wet	No	Yes	No	All	Full	Guide	Yes
London Zoo	Central/North	Fair	Yes	No	No	All	Full	Guide	Yes
Lookout Discovery Park	West	Both	Yes	No	No	All	Full	Yes	Yes
Madame Tussauds/Planetarium	Central	Wet	No	Yes	Yes	All	Part	Guide	Yes
Mill Green Museum & Mill	North	Wet	Yes	No	No	All	No	Guide	No
Mountfitchet Castle	North	Fair	Yes	No	Yes	Part	Part	Guide	Yes
Museum Of London	Central	Wet	Yes	Yes	No	All	Full	Guide	Yes
Museum Of The Moving Image	Central/South	Wet	No	Yes	No	All	Full	Guide	Yes
National Gallery	Central	Wet	No	Yes	No	All	Full	Guide	Yes

National Maritime Museum	East	Wet	Yes	No	Yes	All	Full	Guide	Yes
Natural History Museum	Central	Wet	No	Yes	No	All	Full	Guide	Yes
Odds Farm Park	West	Fair	Yes	No	No	Part	Full	Guide	Yes
Paradise Wildlife Park	North	Fair	Yes	No	No	All	Full	Yes	Yes
Ragged School Museum	East	Wet	Yes	Yes	No	Part	Part	Guide	Yes
Royal Airforce Museum	North	Wet	Yes	Yes	Yes	All	Full	Guide	Yes
Royal Observatory	East	Wet	No	No	Yes	All	Part	Guide	No
Science Museum	Central	Wet	No	Yes	No	All	Full	Guide	Yes
Segaworld	Central	Wet	No	Yes	No	All	Full	Guide	Yes
Tate Gallery	Central	Wet	No	Yes	No	All	Full	Guide	Yes
Thorpe Park	West	Fair	Yes	No	No	Part	Part	Guide	Yes
Tower Of London	Central/East	Both	No	Yes	Yes	All	Part	Guide	No
Verulamium Museum	North	Wet	Yes	No	Yes	All	Full	Guide	No
Waterhall Farm	North	Fair	Yes	No	No	All	Part	Guide	Yes

Attraction	Region	Weather	Car Parking	Tube	Train	Opening Season	Disabled Access	Dogs Allowed?	Restaurant
Westminster Abbey	Central	Wet	No	Yes	No	All	Part	Guide	No
Whipsnade Tree Cathdral	North	Fair	Yes	No	No	All	Full	Yes	No
Whipsnade Wild Animal Park	North	Fair	Yes	No	No	Part	Full	Guide	Yes
Wimpole Hall	North	Both	Yes	No	No	All	Part	Yes	Yes